Praise for *How We Show Up*

"Mia Birdsong is one of our most important thinkers and strategists for how we build structures to support the families that we actually have and the kinds of families we would build if we weren't all so obsessed with respectability. This book gives us both the vision and the blueprint for how to do this in ways that feel sustainable, and quite frankly otherworldly. I left this book feeling some[thing I haven't felt in a] long time: hopeful."

—Brittney Cooper, author of *Eloqu[ent Rage:
A Black Feminist Discovers Her S[uperpower]*

"Mia Birdsong's deeply personal book calls forth a deeply public truth: that we're all better off when we're all better off. Her search for the meaning of community and belonging will inspire Americans from many walks to show up in a new way."

—Eric Liu, CEO of Citizen University and author of *Become America*

"This is the book we've all been waiting for about the 'craft'— and that's what Mia Birdsong so insightfully names it—of creating community. She's a master craftswoman herself— gathering stories of such intentionality, honesty, and reliability that you will immediately start living your life more radically and reaping the rewards."

—Courtney E. Martin, author of *The New Better Off: Reinventing the American Dream*

"This book is a blueprint to being vulnerable enough to love harder, dig deeper, and be unafraid to redefine and expand our relationships. A beautiful and helpful piece of work."

—Tiq Milan, writer and LGBTQ advocate

HOW WE SHOW UP

HOW WE SHOW UP

RECLAIMING FAMILY, FRIENDSHIP, AND COMMUNITY

MIA BIRDSONG

hachette
BOOKS
New York

Hachette Go, an imprint of Hachette Books
Hachette Book Group
1290 Avenue of the Americas
New York, NY 10104
HachetteGo.com
Facebook.com/HachetteGo
Instagram.com/HachetteGo

First Edition: June 2020

Hachette Books is a division of Hachette Book Group, Inc.

The Hachette Go and Hachette Books names and logos are trademarks of Hachette Book Group, Inc.

The publisher is not responsible for websites (or their content) that are not owned by the publisher.

Print book interior design by Trish Wilkinson.

Library of Congress Cataloging-in-Publication Data has been applied for.

ISBNs: 978-1-58005-807-0 (trade paperback), 978-1-58005-806-3 (ebook)

Printed in the United States of America

LSC-C

Printing 7, 2022

For Stella and Solomon
For all our descendants

Without community, there is no liberation.

—AUDRE LORDE

AUTHOR'S NOTE

Names

Our stories of family and relationships are deeply layered. They are sources of love, care, and inspiration. They are also sources of pain, trauma, and rejection. They are intimate, personal, and revealing. People's willingness to share their stories with me for this book is courageous and humbling. Their openness and truth telling is the heart of *How We Show Up*. Understandably, many of them asked me keep their identities between us. Some of the names and details of people's lives have been changed.

Accuracy

Telling other people's stories, particularly when they are folks whose stories often get mistold or erased, comes with tremendous responsibility. I do my best to do it well, accurately, and with care, knowing that I'm learning along the way. Thank you to the people who have helped me move further along by directly or indirectly educating me.

CONTENTS

AKAYA SAID

IN LATE 2018, my mentor Akaya Windwood convened a retreat of about two dozen women of color to contemplate what she called the New Universal, something she and I had started talking about the year before. I had been exploring (and continue to explore) Black women's culture of leadership as an antidote to the damage wrought by the dominance of patriarchy and white supremacy. It's overly binary—Black women versus patriarchy and white supremacy—but was a simple starting point. Akaya expanded it to include women of color more broadly. New Universal is, in part, about redefining what leadership needs to be for us to create a world that is interdependent, generative, and loving. Her invitation was to come together with "like-minded, like-hearted sisters who are dreaming of a world that celebrates, understands, and cherishes our wisdom . . . gathering to create space that is emergent, unstructured, and designed to evoke the best in each of us."

Akaya is a master facilitator, brilliant leader, and believer in infinite possibility. She chose each of the women who attended the four-day gathering, and applied what she calls a "Wise Fools" structure (no agenda or clear outcomes, but an invitation to embrace a "beginner's mind"). I picked up my friend Aisha from the San Francisco Airport and headed north to Petaluma, where the retreat was taking place. On the way, we both admitted our skepticism about this retreat. It seemed like a lot right before the holidays when we both had a million things to take care of. But we were looking at it as an opportunity to spend some time with great folks and have extended solitude to check things off our to-do lists. We agreed that the only reason we'd said yes is because we love and trust Akaya, who is renowned for her ability to develop leaders and her commitment to a just global community infused with purpose and delight. Both of us have been supported, shaped, and encouraged to stand more powerfully in our strengths because of her mentorship. Neither of us could give our husbands any explanation for what we were doing other than when Akaya asks us to do something, we do it. In fact, all Aisha had in her calendar to block out the four days was "Akaya said."

Of course, we were smart to listen to her. What we experienced was extraordinary. Akaya brought all of us together in the mornings and evenings so we could get to know one another and share whatever was on our mind, punctuated with brief free-flowing sermons from her. With little guidance other than "don't do anything you do not fucking want to do," we practiced world making. In the space of four days, we created a culture that was safe, curious, joyful, caring, and generous. We decorated cookies and went for long walks. We discussed our wildest dreams and unspoken desires. We laughed—a lot. We talked—a lot. We cried, sang, and disagreed. We soaked up wisdom, love, and joy in one other's presence.

For sure, it was time out of our regular lives, and there was a suspension of the labor and attention daily life requires.

The retreat center provided our food and shelter. We did not have to tend to the needs of children or elders or anyone else. There were no threats to our well-being that we needed to defend against or navigate. We didn't spend enough time together or get close enough to have any serious conflict. But with very little effort we stepped out of the demands and constraints—external and internal—of our modern lives. We dispensed with the constant rushing and linear ordering of hours and days. We stepped away from the sense that everything from time to money to food to space will run out at any second. We let go of the desire to be right, the fight to be seen and heard, the race toward better and more. We lingered, we listened, we inquired, we wondered. Our rhythm was not driving and relentless, but continually transforming and spacious. We had time to enjoy and learn, to rest and reflect, and to offer and receive care and consideration from one another.

When I returned home, I felt full and inspired by the people I'd met or reconnected with, and encouraged by what we'd done together. I was also keenly aware of the absence of the world we'd made. It was quite clear to me that if the broader culture was closer to a version of what we'd made, everyone would be better off—not just women of color, but everyone. And it made me a little heartbroken to be newly aware of what's possible but absent from the world I regularly live in. For sure, I have bits of it. I have circles of women I gather with regularly. I have taken steps to remove myself from contexts that demand rushing and vying for space to be seen and heard. I am breathing more, challenging my tendency to consume, and encouraging myself to hold abundance in my mind and heart when I'm feeling the panic of scarcity.

But I want more of the world we built—one where we feel seen and accepted, where we feel like we have enough of what we need and can ask for what we want, where we love up and lean on each other. I want to bring the culture of the New Universal into my life and the lives of my loved ones, and ultimately all of us.

James Baldwin wrote, "The place in which I'll fit will not exist until I make it."[1] We all seek belonging, and for very few of us, even the most hermitic, is that place completely separate from others. That means it's something we must build together. As a politically radical Black woman and a curious person, I am committed to living the most liberated life I can with those around me. And I'm not interested in having to step out of my daily life to have it or in creating a separate place in isolation from the rest of the world—that leaves too many people behind. We have to make it where we live.

---

1. Claudia Roth Pierpont, "Another Country," *New Yorker*, February 2, 2009, https://www.newyorker.com/magazine/2009/02/09/another -country.

ONE

When Failure Leads Us Home

The Trap of the American Dream

> A country is only as strong as the people who
> make it up and the country turns into what the
> people want it to become.[1]
>
> —JAMES BALDWIN

THE AMERICAN DREAM is both an illusion and an aspiration. It is a false promise and real potential. It is a jumble of contradictions. The Founding Fathers wrote powerfully about freedom and self-governance while inhabiting stolen land, enslaving people, and excluding most of the population from participating in that self-governance. Today, America is a place where a Black man can be elected president by people who would not hesitate to call the cops on a Black person picking up trash outside their own house, barbecuing in a park, or napping in a dorm. It's a country where we celebrate the extravagance of the superrich collecting cars they will never drive and buying mansions for their horses while

---

1. James Baldwin, "Notes for a Hypothetical Novel," in *Baldwin Collected Essays* (New York: Library of America, 1998), 230.

witnessing whole communities of people living outdoors in tent cities because the cost of housing is unreachably high.

While the American Dream has never been an option for most members of some communities—queer folks, unmarried adults, Black folks, people who grow up poor, just to name a few—it's also overpromised on the satisfaction, contentment, and happiness it delivers to people who do get their piece of it. The people winning at the American Dream are some disconnected, unsatisfied, lonely people.

The American Dream's narrowly defined paths to happiness and success rely on an acceptance of prescribed roles, and a lot of accumulation and exhibition. The quintessential "self-made man" (and it is almost always a man) is self-sufficient, confident, stoic, righteously industrious, performatively heterosexual, and powerful. His success is signified through acquisition—home ownership, marriage, and children—and display of taste and things—craft beer and Courvoisier, Teslas and big trucks, bespoke suits and I-don't-care CEO hoodies. On the surface, it looks like that idea has evolved some. We have our Beyoncés, Baracks, and Buttigiegs. But that doesn't mean the American Dream has become liberated from its origins or that its promise of freedom is more free. It just means more of us are permitted entry to the club if we do the double duty of conforming to its standards and continuing to meet the ones set for us—women must lean in, queer couples must get married, people of color must be master code-switchers.

The American Dream remains defined by whiteness and masculinity, no matter who occupies the role; our most rewarded and celebrated leaders, even if they are not straight white men, exemplify these standards. And because it is held up as the ideal we should all want to achieve, we've all been socialized to reach for it. Perhaps most damaging, it includes a toxic individualism that creates barriers to deep connection and intimacy. When we are oriented toward doing it ourselves and getting ours, we cut ourselves off from the kinds of relationships that can only be built when we allow ourselves to be open and generous.

My work sits at the intersection of race, gender, and class, and has a particular focus on family. My advocacy and activism through organizations like the Economic Security Project, Family Story, and the Family Independence Initiative, and think tanks like the Aspen Institute and New America point toward reframing our understanding of how we achieve the "good life" and who we live it with. In order to be able to tell a reimagined story of what should matter when it comes to family in the United States, I have studied and scrutinized our most accepted versions of "good" and "bad" families. Family holds a place of honor in the American Dream—a "good family" has some of the status of a successful career, but with the added weight of morality and virtue. By American Dream standards, a "good family" is an insular, nuclear family comprising a legally married man and woman raising biological children. This family is self-sufficient—and as such, functions as an independent unit. It's toxic individualism, but in family-unit form. Despite adjustments that have made a little room for same-sex partners who conform to a heteronormative standard, Black people who can live up to a white standard of respectability, and women who do paid labor in addition to the unpaid labor they already shoulder, the model is basically the same. Any deviation from the model is seen as second best or underachieving. Adoption is something you do after pregnancy doesn't work out. Being a single parent only happens when you can't keep or find a partner. Divorce is a failure. A rental is where you live until you've gotten your down payment together. Unmarried couples are asked, "When are you getting married?" We may understand why a couple does not have children, but somehow being child-free confers a lack of completion of, and commitment to, family. Married couples without kids, particularly women, are regularly asked, "When are you going to have kids?" And while a woman might not be considered a failure as a human being if she never marries, she's still seen as a bit sad.

It's not just those of us who have families at or near the top of the hierarchy who hold these perspectives. We all internalize cultural norms, including the people whose lives are belittled or disregarded because of those standards. And we often do see our choices through the lens of society's judgment because we are not separate from society. Even if we intellectually understand the double standards and antiquated values underlying those norms, our heart and gut doesn't always evolve at the same pace. Hell, I have been studying and thinking about all of this for more than two decades and I still catch myself upholding some old story about love, happiness, or success.

Without accessible, celebrated models of what happiness, purpose, connection, and love look like outside the American Dream model, we are pulled in toward it. I feel this tugging all the time. I've achieved just enough of the American Dream that sometimes it has me thinking, *Maybe, just maybe it is for me. Just maybe its security and sparkle are real.* Deviating from the beautifully packaged path can seem reckless and even arrogant. I mean, I have not just myself to consider, but my husband and kids as well. Who the hell am I to question this reward? Sometimes I just want to ignore all the obvious holes in the story, the places where the lies show through the façade, and just let the current take me.

There is a version of my story that makes it easy to hold me up as a poster child of the promise of the American Dream. But the reality has more nuance and is, frankly, a more beautiful truth. I am the only child of an only child on my mother's side. I am a first-generation American on my daddy's side. I am the child of divorce, raised by a single mom. I was poor to working class as a kid. I left home at eighteen and eventually made my way west like colonizing pilgrims, like hopeful fame-seekers, like Black refugees of the Great Migration. I found my American Dream in Oakland, California.

I don't remember as a young child ever wanting to be married to a man, raising children. As a teenager, I remember clearly that I *didn't* want children—I did not like them. I don't remember ever wanting the house, the car, the dog, the career. I remember those Enjoli commercials with the career woman leaning in pre–Sheryl Sandberg—acquiring literal and figurative bacon without emasculating her husband (and smelling lovely the whole time, apparently). I don't know if I didn't think those things were for me, or I truly didn't want them. But one morning, the summer I was twenty-seven, I woke up and as I looked at the ceiling beams above me, I felt both an emotional and physical urge to be a mother. It was like a switch had been flipped and I was filled with a longing that had weight. It felt like falling in love and heartbreak at the same time.

My dream of motherhood didn't shift my idea of family toward the nuclear. It didn't really occur to me to do it with a partner. I was raised by a single mother, but maybe more than that, I am very much an only child and the idea of having to make parenting decisions with another person was unappealing to me. In deciding on pregnancy versus adoption, I chose the latter because sperm cost money. I eventually began readying myself to become a foster-adopt parent. I researched my options, questioned social workers, reviewed forms and pamphlets, did some vague budgeting, and began looking for the kind of housing that the system requires foster parents to have.

And then I met Nino. When I tell this part of our story, I usually say he ruined my plans. I knew within days of meeting him that I would marry him and that complicated my adoption plan and messed up my timeline. But, really he helped me realize something much fuller than I had imagined for myself. I am still sometimes surprised to find myself here living this seemingly quintessential American Dream. We've been married since 2005. We have two biological kids—a girl and a boy. We are entrepreneurs. We own our home. We make enough money to pay for gym memberships, tutors, and the occasional vacation.

But, from the beginning of our lives together, I knew that maintaining and continuing to develop my chosen family and my community was not only how I would get my needs met, but how my marriage and my kids would be supported. Ours is not the insular, self-sufficient nuclear family. We have created some of the sense of safety, belonging, and care we all need—not just with the four of us, but with others. Our family is made up of chosen, adopted, and biological aunties, grandparents, siblings, uncles, and cousins. Further, we have a community of friends and neighbors that provide both safety net and spring board—support when things are hard, and celebration when things are especially good. We, in turn, provide those things for them.

All that said, it is hard and not quite enough. I struggle with the cultural push toward insularity and self reliance. I suffer from the inertia of screens and the ennui of stuff. I indulge in the brief hit of dopamine comfort that comes from online shopping (the kitchen gadgets, the houseplants, the skincare products). I drink wine to unwind. I sip from the warm cup of promised safety and comfort the American Dream serves up even though I know it's a lie. The closer I get to the mirage of security and achievement and the more trappings of capitalism I acquire, the harder it is to resist.

But I do have examples to reach for when I find myself floundering. Growing up, I had models of how to do family and community in ways that are expansive, that provide safety and security through love and commitment, not money and alarm systems. I had sketches of blueprints that showed me how family can be built, not just from blood and law, but shared experience and values, from love that looks like a million things.

My mother, an only child, was orphaned at a young age. What little family she did have disowned her when she married my father (she is a white woman from Macon, Georgia; he was a Black man from Jamaica). My parents split up when I was three. My dad moved a few states away to go to law school and the rest of his family was in Jamaica or Canada. I saw him and them once or twice a year and regularly talked with my dad on the phone, but in terms of consistent, present support, we were without family. So, my mom patched together community for us. I remember a Thanksgiving at her English professor's home and a week living with friends when my mom had knee surgery. I had a trio of aunties—Melanie, Lisa, and Dorothy—made up of her closest friends. We joined the Jewish Community Center because they had a single parents group (we are not Jewish). With them, we did things like have potlucks, go on camping trips, and celebrate holidays. She made sure we knew our neighbors and the important details of their lives. That meant that when I got home after school and forgot my keys, I had places to stay until she got home from work.

I built family and community for myself starting in my late teens. I built it out of childhood friends and people I worked with. I built it out of people I met at bars and shows and protests. I built it out of friends of friends. Actually, it's inaccurate to say *I* built it. One person does not build family or a community. While I can claim my deliberate effort, everyone who is part of my circles participated in their creation—actively or passively, they built with me.

For many years, part of the economic justice work I've done has focused on shifting the public narrative around poverty and people who are poor. By using a combination of data and storytelling, I shine a light on the resilience, creativity, knowledge, and capability that exists in low-income communities. In doing this, I counter a narrative that blames people for being poor instead of recognizing both the assets of poor communities and the systemic barriers people are up against. One of the things I focus on is how people who are poor often leverage social capital to mitigate their experience of poverty. Or, to put it more plainly, how connected people help one another out.

Sometimes this is relying on practical support, like when friends pitch in to help with things like home repairs, childcare, and haircuts, instead of paying for it the way middle- or upper-class people are likely to do. Sometimes it is the emotional support people lean on to get through hard times. When I give talks or presentations, I tell anecdotes: A trio of women who created a cleaning business together so they could collectively care for their children while earning money for their families. A mom who got support in raising a child with learning disabilities by starting a parents group for other families with children who have learning disabilities. A man who got his neighbors together to transform the neglected, empty lot across the street from his house into a community green space.

The audiences I speak in front of are full of policy makers, government officials, think tank leaders, and nonprofit executives—people who, by American standards of success, have made it. But inevitably, after my talk or presentation, one of them—almost always a white man—will come to talk to me afterward, waiting until others have asked their questions, and tell me they wish they had in their own lives the kind of community I described.

It's not that these folks don't have friends and family. They do. They have spouses and children. They have people with whom they have dinner or sometimes go on vacation. But something about their lives leaves them feeling lonely.

They are not alone in feeling lonely. There is a wide and growing body of research on how lonely and disconnected people in America are from their friends and from their neighbors. A 2018 survey from Cigna found that a quarter of us don't have people in our lives who we feel understand us.[2]

---

2. "Cigna 2018 U.S. Loneliness Index," accessed February 18, 2020, https://www.cigna.com/assets/docs/newsroom/loneliness-survey-2018 -fact-sheet.pdf.

Only half of us have daily meaningful interactions with others. "At least two in five surveyed sometimes or always feel as though they lack companionship (43%), that their relationships are not meaningful (43%), that they are isolated from others (43%), and/or that they are no longer close to anyone (39%)."[3] Only 26 percent of us know most of our neighbors.[4] A third of us have never even interacted with our neighbors.[5]

Not having deep connection is causing us mental and physical harm. Vivek Murthy, former surgeon general of the United States, wrote in the *Harvard Business Review* that "Loneliness and weak social connections are associated with a reduction in lifespan similar to that caused by smoking 15 cigarettes a day."[6] A meta-analysis from the Association for Psychological Science warns that loneliness and social isolation significantly decrease length of life.[7]

The American Dream version of success can also damage our ability to relate to others. In an article from the *Atlantic* called "Power Causes Brain Damage,"[8] John Useem cites

3. "Cigna 2018 U.S. Loneliness Index."

4. Kim Parker et al., "How Urban, Suburban, and Rural Residents Interact with Their Neighbors," Pew Research Center, May 22, 2018, https://www.pewsocialtrends.org/2018/05/22/how-urban-suburban -and-rural-residents-interact-with-their-neighbors/.

5. Joe Cortright, "Less in Common," City Observatory, September 6, 2015, http://cityobservatory.org/less-in-common/.

6. Vivek Murthy, "Work and the Loneliness Epidemic," *Harvard Business Review,* September 28, 2017, https://hbr.org/cover-story/2017/09 /work-and-the-loneliness-epidemic.

7. Julianne Holt-Lunstad et al., "Loneliness and Social Isolation as Risk Factors for Mortality: A Meta-analytic Review," *Perspectives on Psychological Science* 10, no. 2 (2015): 227–237.

8. Jerry Useem, "Power Causes Brain Damage," *Atlantic,* July/August 2017.

the work of Dacher Keltner, a professor of psychology at UC Berkeley, who found that people in positions of power become "less adept at seeing things from other people's point of view." And what is the American Dream if it is not attaining power? Useem goes on to relay findings from McMaster University neuroscientist Sukhvinder Obhi, who found that power "impairs a specific neural process, 'mirroring,'" that may be the cornerstone of empathy. The more successful we become, the harder it may be for us to connect with others not only because we've developed the habits of toxic individualism in order to succeed, but because we have rewired our brain.

This thing where white men confessed to me their lack of community happened consistently for a few years, but I didn't give it much thought—until one of these men asked me a question. This man, probably in his early thirties, walked toward me after a talk I'd given. He clearly wanted to say something to me, but kept politely gesturing others ahead of him because whatever he had to say, he did not want to say it in anyone's presence. He began like others had, confessional in his admission that he lacked the kind of connection and community I talked about. He made it clear that he had friends, but when he compared his relationships to the ones I'd spoken of, it felt lacking. I nodded in understanding.

But then he asked me *how* to create community and family. I asked him a few questions and gave him a handful of ideas. In the days that followed, I found myself thinking about our conversation, and it made me uncomfortable and unsettled because, as I finally admitted to myself, I should have said, "I don't know." The answer I'd given him was pat and inadequate because the truth was, I couldn't really answer his question.

It was then that I started to see that the more "successful" I became, the harder it was for me to carve out the time that building connection demands, and the less I prioritized deepening relationships. The more uncomfortable I became with being vulnerable and authentic—sharing my flaws, struggles, and fears—the more I felt the need to keep on my armor and present the most together, bad-ass, and brilliant version of myself.

As much as I have witnessed beautiful, strong, interdependent community and expansive, connected family, I have yet to really pull it off the way I truly want. In the last several years, I've felt both agitated and excited about what might be possible. I've felt an energizing desire to be more explicit about the life I'm building. And I want to build that life in deep alignment with my best self's values, and a vision of the world I want to help create.

But what does it really mean to be in deep, close community? What form does it take? Who is included and why? How much of my life do I have to let go of to make room for the kinds of relationships I want? How far and deep must the reach of my heart extend? Can I hold in the light of generosity those who would wish me harm? And what cost is not too much to do so?

Figuring all of this out feels particularly urgent right now, for me personally, for the people I love and care about, and for the future America that I hope for. There is something untenably severed in America right now. I don't mean the "division and divisiveness" so many pundits and thought leaders are lamenting. Those divisions—of class, race, and gender, of values and priorities—have been here for a long time. Now they are just more apparent to more people. What

I'm speaking of is our ability to hold space for one another, to empathize, to make time for connection, to care for one another, to be part of one another's lives.

The American Dream's focus on getting ahead is a race to win so you don't lose. It plays into our well-developed fear instincts, creating a real and imagined scarcity of resources, time, and money. This fear-based sense of scarcity pits us against one another. It also leaves us with a poorly developed sense of "enough," both of the material and of love and care. Both surviving these divisions and perpetuating them is draining us of our emotional resilience, grounding, and breathing room. It has us severing the bonds of empathy that allow us to recognize our shared experiences and our shared fates. This is not to say that there is not a lot of difference and disagreements between and among us. But when we understand those differences as inherently threatening, then we have let that fear allow us to dehumanize other people.[9]

The search for answers to fix our broken experience of community has some people looking backward to the kind of sugar-borrowing and porch-sitting closeness they believe existed in the 1950s. But that was somewhat imaginary and it doesn't work in the context of modern life. We need a vision of community that is relevant and future-facing. A vision that brings us closer to one another, allows us to be vulnerable and imperfect, to grieve and stumble, to be held accountable and loved deeply. We need models of success and leadership that fundamentally value love, care, and generosity of resources and spirit.

---

9. To be clear, I'm not talking about building deep connection with people whose moral compass is broken or who don't respect your basic humanity.

WHAT WE LONG FOR

All of us have ancestral memory of what it's like to live connected, interdependent lives. We may be cut off or too far away from those traditions to claim them, but we can listen to our needs, our longings, and through ritual, rite, and practice build a way of being in the world that honors and makes tangible our connections to one another, to nature, and to spirit.

This is a process of decolonization. Whether you are the descendants of colonizers or the colonized—or, like me, both—all of our peoples have experienced the loss of something essential to our liberated well-being. Whether that was taken from you or given away in the bargain to win power, it is loss. Even if you are a more recent immigrant to America, you likely have your own colonization story. And navigating the American landscape means swimming in its slick of genocide, slavery, destruction, and extraction. All of us have something to shed, something to purge, so we can make room for the reclamation and reinvention of community and family.

Creating relationships and connection outside the arrangements that our current culture presents to us can be exciting and liberating. We get to be creative, coming up with new ways to understand our connections to others and new ways of connecting. We get to throw out what we've learned to want and discover what we actually want and need. We get to uncover ways of belonging and loving that we didn't see before.

But it can also be painful for a whole host of obvious and not-so-obvious reasons. We may encounter internal and external barriers. And if you're like me, it's easy to question everything to a disorienting degree that pushes you toward an abyss of nothingness. What pulls me away from that edge is understanding not just what expansive connection can look like, but what needs we all want met. We find our way back to ourselves—making more clear what our truth is—by listening to the deep longing in our own heart.

We long to be known

We spend a lot of time convincing ourselves and others that we are good people, that we are the best version of ourselves. Part of how we do this is by presenting the world with a curated, if not ideal, rendering of lives. Even without social media, we are selective about the version of us others get to see. We craft stories that highlight our successes and strength, and leave out the places we feel stuck or lost. And sometimes, because we are clever, we present our struggles too, but with their inherent dissonance muted for our audience.

We also engage in the internal strategy of defensively differentiating ourselves from others (by judging, disparaging, comparing) so we can see ourselves as whatever we think they are not (hardworking, moral, enlightened) or beating ourselves up for all the ways we think we're failing and fucking up. But no one is all one thing. We are not the worst things about us, nor are we the best things. We are all capable of harm and bad decisions. We are all capable of love and care. We have all been hurt and experienced loss. We all have successes and things we are good at.

This inability to be vulnerable by being our real, uneven selves creates distance inside us, and between us and others.

But we long to be known, not just for our wins or talents or the good we do in the world, not just for how we overcome hardship, but for our pain and struggle while we are suffering, for our failures and shortcomings. We want to be known so we can be accepted and loved just because we are here. We all want to be enough.

We long to give and receive support

So many of us have a deep aversion to asking for help. The idea of asking for help makes us feel like a failure, makes us feel weak. We often think of needing help as a burden. But that is toxic individualism talking! It's telling us that we should be able to do it on our own, that if we were strong enough, good enough, and capable enough, we wouldn't need help.

So, we struggle mightily to do it alone, to prove ourselves to an unrealistic and unhealthy standard, when reaching out could make our lives not only easier, but better. And we know this. We tell our struggling friends to let us know if they need anything, we tell them to call or text if they want to talk. We help them move, practice saying something hard, bring them food when they are sick (and when they are well), and just listen.

Because the thing is, we love to help. Our best self gets a positive feeling from supporting others. It's a feeling that is not about the gratitude we receive or the points we earn, but an alignment with love and care that fills us. When we see someone experience relief or ease or happiness because we helped them, we are filled. It also reminds us that we are not out here alone, we don't achieve or thrive, or survive or get by, on our own.

Amoretta Morris, a wise woman I know who is rethinking philanthropy, wrote, "It's okay to ask for help. In fact, by doing so, you are taking part in the divine circle of giving and receiving. While we often focus on what the request means for the asker/recipient, we should remember that giving can be transformative for the helper. . . . By not asking for help when you need it, you are blocking that flow."[10]

"By not asking for help when you need it, you are blocking that flow." This is one of the most liberating things I've ever read. We have a responsibility to each other to ask for help when we need it. Instead of listening to the fictitious lone wolf in us, we must listen to the wolf in the pack, and tap into the impulse that moves us to cocreate opportunities for mutuality, opportunities to care for and be there for one another.

We long for freedom and accountability

Both of these ideas are laden and loaded. Our most common understanding of them requires some evolving in this context.

The American Dream tells us that freedom is the state of being unburdened and unconstrained by others or systems. It's about having choices and being able to fully express ourselves. It's having the power to be who we want, go where we want, and do what we want. But we tend to understand it as an individualistic concept. This is where we have to expand our understanding to fold in what is actually an older understanding of freedom.

In *Liberty and Freedom*, David Hackett Fischer explains that the word *free* is derived from the Indo-European *friya*,

10. Amoretta Morris, Facebook post, September 12, 2015.

which means "beloved." *Friend* also shares this common root with *freedom*. A free person was someone who was "joined to a tribe of free people by ties of kinship and rights of belonging."[11] Freedom was the idea that together we can ensure that we all have the things we need—love, food, shelter, safety. The way I've come to understand it, freedom is both an individual and collective endeavor—a multilayered process, not a static state of being. Being free is, in part, achieved through being connected.

Our thinking about accountability has to expand as well. We often think of it as a system of punishment that's meant to keep us from messing up. And if we mess up, we feel ashamed and feel like apologizing. It's a responsibility to others. Accountability, as I mean it, is more about ourselves in the context of the collective. It's seeing the ways we cause hurt or harm as actions that indicate we are not living in alignment with values that recognize our own humanity or the humanity of others. It's about recognizing when our behavior is out of alignment with our best selves. And as Mia Mingus, who you'll read about in Chapter 8, explained to me, you can't hold another person accountable. You can support someone's accountability, but we hold ourselves accountable.

Accountability is also about recognizing and accepting that we are necessary and wanted. It's understanding that when we neglect ourselves, don't care for ourselves, or are not working to live as our best selves, we are devaluing the time, energy, and care that our loved ones offer us.

---

11. David Hackett Fischer, *Liberty and Freedom: A Visual History of America's Founding Ideas* (New York: Oxford University Press, 2005), 5.

This idea of accountability, like many of the things I cover in this book, exists in a gray area that asks us to examine what we have control over and what we don't; what is our responsibility, versus what is our fault; who is the victim and who is the perpetrator. The truth is, we need to discard many of those binaries. One of the many things I learned from the people whose stories are in this book is that sometimes those ideas are not static. We will benefit from giving ourselves and others the benefit of the doubt as we navigate our understanding of ourselves and of others. We need to reach for grace as we weave in and out of what is me and what is you, and what is us.

We exist, not as wholly singular, autonomous beings, nor completely merged, but in a fluctuating space in between. This idea was expressed beautifully in Desmond Tutu's explanation of the South African concept of Ubuntu. He said, "It is to say, my humanity is caught up, is inextricably bound up, in yours. We belong in a bundle of life. We say a person is a person through other persons. It is not I think therefore I am. It says rather: I am human because I belong, I participate, and I share."[12]

"WE THE PEOPLE"

With these words, the drafters of the US Constitution established the idea of a self-governed union—one built and ruled by its residents. But when they wrote "people," the founders did not actually mean all residents of the United States. They

12. Desmond Tutu, *No Future Without Forgiveness* (New York: Crown, 2009), 31.

were thinking about people whose class, race, and gender matched their own.

But thanks to the people they left out (and a few good accomplices), progress has moved us closer to realizing the aspirational sentiment of their words, instead of being limited by their intentions. It is that—the ability and desire so many of us have to make America better than intended, to improve upon what those who came before us did, planned, or even imagined—that is what we should recognize as the American Dream. Because a dream is an imagined reality, it is about bringing something into existence that wasn't here before. As Baldwin wrote, "A country is only as strong as the people who make it up and the country turns into what the people want it to become."[13]

We are witnessing a shift right now. A stale version of the American Dream is crumbling, breaking apart, and being discarded as a new version emerges. People are widening the narrow roles they've been assigned. Many of us are refusing to feel guilty or shameful for not following convention when it comes to success or building family and community. Many of us are moving through the grief that comes from letting go of the picture we had of what our lives would look like so we can make room for a different, and maybe even better, picture. More of us are creating new (to us) and reimagined models.

These ways of creating relationships, family, and community are, of course, not actually new. What is new is that people who are following unconventional paths are more public, are documenting their experiences, and are able to find one another more easily (thank you, internet).

---

13. Baldwin, "Notes for a Hypothetical Novel," 230.

Part of the essence of this shifting is that connection is not about a particular structure, it's about values and love and care. It's about the things that provide what we long for, whatever form that takes. It's about pulling apart the boundaries of what love and friendship look like, what romantic partnership is and provides, and who counts as family. It's about finding your people and redefining who "your people" is.

It's in communities like the ones you'll read about in this book that we can find proof that another world is not just possible, but is emerging all around us. The places that I've found the strongest, most expansive, boundary-bending, inclusive examples of family and community are among the people who experience the most adversity and oppression, the people who have always been at the forefront of progress in America. Poor people, queer people, Black people, unhoused people— especially the women and gender-nonconforming people among them—to varying degrees operate outside convention because convention has rejected us. People do not survive racism, xenophobia, gender discrimination, and poverty without developing extraordinary skills, systems, and practices of support. And in doing so, they carve a path for everyone else.

I want to point more deeply toward Blackness and queerness here because it is from Black folks and queer folks, especially queer Black women, that I have learned the most.

The gift of Blackness is an expansive notion of family— family beyond blood and law, "play cousins," and "fictive kin." It's finding home in multiple houses, defying patriarchy and marriage; it's stay-at-home dads, and coparenting. Many of the things that are becoming more acceptable—desirable, even—and mainstream when it comes to family are practices Black people in America have been doing for hundreds of years. Despite attempts to keep us from one another, despite false accusations of brokenness and dysfunction, we have insisted on making family with whomever we love—or even dislike but feel responsible for.

Then there's the gift of queerness. As poet Brandon Wint wrote in a much-quoted social media post several years ago, "Not queer like gay; queer like escaping definition. Queer like some sort of fluidity and limitlessness all at once. Queer like a freedom too strange to be conquered. Queer like the fearlessness to imagine what love can look like, and to pursue it."[14] There is a long history of queer folks staying open to the infinite ways that love, romance, family, and friendship can manifest while straight people adhered to a handful of options.

This is not to gloss over the harm done by systems of oppression and exclusion. But it is to recognize the elevation that exists despite the oppression people experience. There are folks who, at great cost, just by insisting on existence and self-definition, have created more room for the rest of us to be expansive and self-determined in our identities and relationships. We owe a debt to those who have challenged the norms our culture has defined for us—norms that limit who we can be, how we present ourselves, how we love, who we call family.[15]

I wrote this book because I'm looking for connection, love, and care that is beyond the confines and the defaults and

---

14. Brandon Wint, Facebook post, February 6, 2014.

15. I want to be clear here that when you benefit from the work others have done, especially when you—by nature of your identity or access to resources—hold more power and privilege than they do, you have a responsibility to show up for them. That's the rule. It's not one I can enforce, but I can tell you about it and make clear that I think you're an asshole if you reject the idea of following it.

norms of my upbringing, the dominant culture, and my own awareness. This book was made as I was in an active phase of exploring all of these ideas and issues—a process that began before I started writing and will no doubt continue long after you read it. The way I talk about relationships, gender, love, intimacy, and so many other things has evolved since I started thinking about them, and it will continue to evolve. As I wrote, I had the familiar feeling of struggling to reach past the edges of my understanding toward something more aligned with the truth I wanted to grasp and articulate. There is excitement and discomfort in that, which I tried to embrace as gracefully as I could.

In making this book, I talked with hundreds of people and formally interviewed nearly sixty. The stories I share with you are snapshots of their thinking and their lives when I spoke to them. But our lives and the relationships in them evolve and shift. What was true for them when they spoke with me may not be true when you read this. Perhaps that goes without saying, but I think it's worth pointing out because it sits so squarely inside what I explore in this book.

As with all things centered on people and relationship, nothing we create together with our whole selves, our baggage and damage, our dreams and passions, is going to be clear or static or definitive. Not only are there not limited ways of creating family and community, but there are not limited ways of staying family and community. It's all mutable and evolving. From this book, I hope you get a picture of what's possible, ideas for creating connection that are broader and deeper than what you previously thought, a reflection of what you already have lifted up and celebrated, or an affirmation of what you already practice.

TWO

Me and Us

Self-Care in the Context of Community

Notice you. Notice you among us.
— AKAYA WINDWOOD

FAMILY AND COMMUNITY can and should be where we find belonging, care, and love. But they are often also the source of our deepest wounds and our greatest damage. So, it is not without pause that I praise and celebrate family and community as safety and salvation. We all have the capacity to hurt as well as the capacity to love, we have the power to diminish and lift up, to harm and heal. And inevitably, we run the spectrum of these intentions and actions, often with the same people (on the same damn day). Each person in our orbit has their gifts and growing edges. Each person is a variable that can change—shifting the makeup of the whole. Our trauma, wounds, and baggage add volatility. So, we must be present to the work of collective transformation out of pain and damage toward healing and growth.

I've come to understand that the things I want to do to be my best self and live my best life are also necessary for me to be in workable relationships with others. That means self-care, self-reflection, healing, and evolving. It means tapping into tremendous compassion—for others and ourselves—as we journey. It means committing to our own evolution, and supporting the evolution of our loved ones as they support us.

This work we have to do is also about reorienting ourselves around what it means to be an individual. Our individuality is entwined with our connectedness; so the work of healing and growth happens both alone and in relation to others. We are the only ones who can decide we will heal and grow, but it's a collective process.

The American Dream is a clusterfuck of intersecting oppressions that function systemically and infect us individually. Capitalism, patriarchy, and white supremacy (all of which create offshoots like ableism, transphobia, ageism, and others) are embedded in the systems and institutions we all interact with—everything from housing to health care to media to jobs to education.[1] But they are also embedded in each of us.

The work of recognizing and excavating the toxicity of the American Dream each of us has inside of us is lifelong work. It is work we must do alongside the specifically personal work of dealing with things like the fact that your father was critical or your mother was withholding, or your uncle sexually assaulted you or you experienced abandonment as a child. These wounds—the specifically personal and the systemically personal—are intertwined.

My calling to work toward social justice feels fundamentally joyful. But managing the impact of external and

---

1. There are lots of schools of thought on how to think about various forms of oppression and their origins. Some would argue that capitalism creates all of them, some would argue that there is a whole reinforcing web of dozens of kinds of oppression. The way I've articulated it is what currently makes sense to me.

internalized oppression is both something I'm used to and something that exhausts and breaks my heart.

It's a lot. And let me be clear about something. Not only is it not easy and not our fault, it's not fair. It's not fair that we inherit all this baggage, but (as I remind my children when they get different-size pieces of cake), shit is not fair. We can certainly rail against what is unfair (things like hypercritical parents, not cake), and fight against injustice (things like racism, not cake). But at the end of the day, we—each one of us—are the only ones who can decide we are going to suffer less in the face of the wrongs we have experienced and continue to experience. We can decide that our own experience of contentment, pleasure, and liberation is ultimately more important than being pissed about the fact that we shouldn't have to deal with it in the first place.

It can be hard to walk the line between claiming our agency to lessen our pain and suffering, and blaming ourselves if we don't. Our anger and hurt are legitimate. I find relief in realizing that I don't have to stay mad at the injustices or cruelties I experience for them to be wrong. The way forward is for us to build the life and love that gives us purpose and well-being. In order to do that, we have to do some hard labor to expel the harmful inheritance we've internalized.

Being on the receiving end of harmful oppressions is decidedly and specifically horrible. But wielding them has its own corrupting and denigrating impact on the imposer. This is important to understand, not because it makes those who hold privilege and power "victims" or somehow as equally harmed as those who experience racism, sexism, and classism. It's important to understand because the work of dismantling systems of oppression that you benefit from isn't altruistic work that just helps others; it is about your own liberation as well.

American capitalism extracts from poor and middle-class people and from our planet, and builds detachment and greed in the hearts of the wealthy. Patriarchy hurts women and gender-nonconforming people, and it also deeply limits men. White supremacy harms people of color, and it also diminishes white people.[2] I'm going to repeat this, because I want to be irrefutably clear, *the harm experienced by the oppressors is not equivalent to the harm experienced by the oppressed.* Capitalism, white supremacy, and patriarchy are not good for anyone, but the work that needs to be done by those who exert oppression and those who are the targets is markedly different.

While the corrupting power of capitalism on rich people and the restrictive nature of patriarchy on men is fairly apparent, white supremacy's negative impact on white people is underexplored and warrants some unpacking. Even pointing that out makes me uncomfortable because white people exploring the harm of white supremacy on themselves should not prioritize that over the work they must do to end the way

---

2. One of the unfortunate unintended consequences of the civil rights movement is that it cloaked racism in the robe of the Klansman and their brand of extremism. It means the spectrum of racism a white person can hold and practice is understood as open hostility and hate, leaving little room for discussion and reckoning of microagressions, bias (unconscious or otherwise), and harmful but less vitriolic racism. White folks get defensive when they are confronted with their racism because they associate it with segregationists and burning crosses. So let's just be clear here. If you're a white person who grew up in America (or any number of other countries), you benefit from white supremacy and hold racists views. That doesn't make you a bad person—none of us are all bad or all good; it does mean you have some work to do to reduce the harm racism causes people of color and to free yourself.

it harms people of color. But I also agree that what Lama Rod Owens calls "the trauma of whiteness"[3] is not going to be wholly healed without white people recognizing that they have work to do on themselves that includes understanding how their own liberation is impeded by white supremacy.

When we hear "white supremacy," we tend to think of the blatant, visible racism of the Klansman, the N-word, or the modern-day Nazis. I'm focused on the more mundane and insidious white supremacy that is embedded in American cultures, systems, institutions, the dynamics of relationships, and our own psyches. As Tema Okun points out in her piece "White Supremacy Culture," "Culture is powerful precisely because it is so present and at the same time so very difficult to name or identify."[4] It's the pervasiveness, and sometimes near-invisibility, of white supremacy that makes it both hard to pull apart and toxic.

There are a variety of downsides to white supremacy for white people. There's the proximate harm of having people of color you may love be harmed by white supremacy. There are also contributions from people of color we are collectively missing out on because white supremacy creates barriers for people of color's brilliance. There's the soul-deadening impact of having an identity that is predicated on the oppression

3. Rev. angel Kyodo Williams and Lama Rod Owens with Jasmine Syedullah, *Radical Dharma: Talking Race, Love, and Liberation* (Berkeley, CA: North Atlantic Books, 2016), 156–157.
4. I highly recommend reading this piece from Kenneth Jones and Tema Okun: *Dismantling Racism: A Workbook for Social Change Groups*, http://www.dismantlingracism.org/, to further understand what white supremacy looks like. https://collectiveliberation.org/wp-content/uploads/2013/01/White_Supremacy_Culture_Okun.pdf.

of other people. My friend Courtney (who is white) told me, "I think of it as a festering wound at the center of our lives—this deep knowing that the country and by extension our own lives have been built on the backs of others."

The American Dream is white supremacy culture bound up with capitalism and patriarchy. In addition to espousing a belief that white people are superior to people of color, white supremacy is also a culture of rigidity, efficiency, more-is-better, ignorance-is-bliss, scarcity hoarding, binaries, and toxic individualism. My friend Matt (also white) spoke to how it limits his ability to connect with others. "White supremacy makes it harder for white folks to connect authentically, understand others, and accurately empathize. Since oppression is definitionally a form of dehumanization, since it denies the full subjecthood of those being oppressed, I think there's a deep level in which it limits human connection." It keeps white people from being deeply known—to others and themselves. It casts what is human about white people as weakness.

SHOWING UP FOR OURSELVES

The personal work we do to reject American Dreamism and create more well-being in our lives is necessary, not only for our own selves, but for our relationships. Taking care of ourselves and addressing our baggage helps us have workable relationship with, and care for, others.

I can better support the people in my life if my own well-being is tended to. I am a better parent, partner, and friend when I engage in regular emotional hygiene and I'm not leaking all over the people around me. I can be more

present for my community when I'm well rested and caring
for my body. When I get sloppy about sleep, exercise, nutrition, relaxation, and any number of things that support my
physical and emotional well-being, I'm not as kind, patient,
or available to my loved ones. That means I have to show up
for myself first.

If you're like me, you sometimes get eye-rolly or anxious
at the mention of self-care. Its popularity speaks to the deep
need we have for practices that allow us to support our own
wellness. But it's been co-opted by capitalism as a thing you
need equipment, apps, and retreats to practice. It's also been
diluted to focus on things like eating ice cream and binging
on TV.

Deanna Zandt created a comic called "The Unspoken
Complexity of Self-Care" to clarify distinctions about self-
care. According to her, ice cream and TV would fall under
"self-soothing." These are things that "provide distraction
and/or comfort in difficult times." Things like therapy, setting and keeping boundaries, and meditating fall under the
heading of "self-care," which are things that "help you find
meaning, and support your growth and groundedness."[5]

We know what we are "supposed" to do—eat more vegetables and move our body, practice mindfulness, rest and get
enough sleep, address mental and physical health issues, deal
with our unresolved shit. All of which is nearly impossible in

_____

5. There are two other categories Deanna illustrates: Community care,
"workarounds for systems that inherently support care (i.e., capitalism)"
like co-housing and multiple forms of intimate relationships, is much
of what you'll read about in this book. Structural care is "systems that
support community care, self-care, and self-soothing" like living wage,
guaranteed income, and universal health care.

the culture created by the American Dream, which sucks up our time, doesn't adequately resource most of us, and makes many of these supports inaccessible. If you're Black, queer, or have a disability, for example, the pool of care providers who have the necessary awareness to understand your experience, much less avoid doing damage, is very small. (The racist therapist horror stories people, including me, have are truly awful.) If you're working or learning full-time (or both) and/or caretaking for anyone, or have a disability for which your access needs are often not met, the time you have to cook, exercise, or sleep is minimal. Access to things like health care, therapy, and fresh produce are largely dependent on how much money you have and where you live. It is expensive to be well.

Self-care can also just be another thing you procrastinate on and feel shitty about not doing. It can be another bullet on our to-do list, or a mask—Think positive thoughts! Document your gratitude!—that hides our messiness from ourselves and others. It is also some shamey, disingenuous bullshit to be told that if we practice deep breathing or detox from sugar, we'll find some ease when the pain and exhaustion we're feeling is mostly perpetuated by our culture. Your getting in your steps doesn't make the hardship of experiencing systemic oppression or the energy suck of capitalism go away.

But if the alternative is just succumbing to feeling like garbage, that's also not an answer. Because we very much want to better manage stress, fatigue, depression, and anxiety. We want to feel good in our body. We want to feel good about ourselves and our lives, and to create more room for rest, joy, and pleasure. I think we have to try to build a stronger shield

against systems of oppression and work to lessen the damage
they do. And since no one is coming to save us, I've found
that the most effective path forward is with others who need
these same supports.

BLACK WOMEN'S FREEDOM CIRCLE

Women have been circling formally and informally probably
forever. Around fires, in covens, red tents, church basements,
and kitchens, we gather to share advice, tell our truths, cast
spells, pass on news and knowledge, witness and be seen, find
comfort and solidarity, plan and conspire, and get shit done.

My mother-in-love, Jacque, has been part of interlock-
ing and overlapping circles of women for more than forty
years. Her circles have been an escape from the grind of daily
life, a source of learning and growth, and support through
hard times. The first time she had cancer, her circle held her
through it. "These women's circles are an ancient process and
we reach for that," she told me. "They've been a way for me
to become who I am."

I went to one of her circles when my daughter, Stella, was
a little over one year old. It was at "The Nest," a one-room
cabin near Jacque's home in the Sierra foothills of California. The gatherings always include some ceremony—a kind
of mash-up of religious and spiritual traditions—music and
food and wine. There was deep and powerful conversation
and a tremendous amount of laughing.

That evening, after a day of art making, soaking in a
wood-heated hot tub (a dozen or so naked, proud, post-
menopausal women is a beautiful sight), and delicious food,
I snuggled Stella in a sleeping bag on the porch and we fell

asleep watching the bats swooping just above our head and
listening to the riotous cackling of the women inside. I felt
like I'd been anointed.

I now have my own circles of women. The first was the
least intentional. I met Brooke and Allie at our mutual friend
Amanda's birthday party in 2002. A couple of years later,
after Amanda and I each had our first kid, we began getting
together regularly. Our time together is mostly spent catching each other up on life—more kids, Allie went through
grad school, Brooke became a midwife, romances and break-
ups. We sometimes have a project—making sauerkraut or lip
balm. Sometimes we go for a hike or picnic. We talk about
our values and approaches to everything from parenting to
conflict. Like Jacque's circles, there is food and wine, sadness, care, and laughter.

In July 2015, my new-at-the-time friend Courtney invited me to a potluck gathering of women at her house. She
sent an invitation that opened with this gem from Margaret
Wheatley:

> Real listening always brings people closer together.
> Trust that meaningful conversations can change your
> world.
> Rely on human goodness. Stay together.[6]

The email continued, "For a while now I've been hungry
for a space and time where I can be with women I think are

---

6. Margaret Wheatley, *Turning to One Another: Simple Conversations to
Restore Hope to the Future* (San Francisco: Berrett-Koehler, 2002).

brilliant and kind and have complex, deep conversation. I want to learn from you. I want to hear myself into my own wisdom." The topic of our first gathering would be ambition. In a follow-up email, she sent some optional short readings and videos to get us thinking about it before we met. We've met every month since then.

In this circle, we always have a topic of discussion—sexual harassment, ego, giving fewer fucks, guilt, sex, creativity—and a facilitator. That roll has largely fallen on Courtney, but a few of us have taken turns. Two years in, when Twilight facilitated our conversation about anger, I realized how much safety we'd built. We'd moved from talking about our feelings to sometimes being *in* our feelings. This circle is not a tight-knit group of friends. Some of us are close to others, but there are also people in the group who never see the others outside these gatherings. But following the ancient tradition of women's circles, we have collectively created a space that is safe enough for us to talk about things that are hard even though the conversations are more intellectual. And we laugh a lot.

Both of these groups are a refreshing breath, an opportunity to get deep both personally and intellectually.

If those groups are a breath, Black Women's Freedom Circle is an exhalation. Sometimes it's the sigh you make when you lower yourself into a warm bath, sometimes it's the scream you've been holding in for fear of falling apart, sometimes it's the praise song that rises in your chest from love or joy or validation.

Black Women's Freedom Circle (BWFC) also has its origins in July 2015. I arrived at Lake Merritt United Methodist Church hopeful but emotionally heavy. So many Black women who were in my orbit were dying, being diagnosed with debilitating diseases, or managing chronic illness. I was leveling up my own self-care, but recognized that the daily stresses of racism and sexism take their toll, no matter what.

I was at the church to participate in a retreat put together by Movement Strategy Center, an Oakland-based organization that helps build social movements. The retreat was part of their Transitions Lab, which brought together activists and organizers from several social justice fields to imagine and plan the future we want to create. We explored what we needed individually and collectively to create that vision. During a long break, I took a walk with Nwamaka Agbo, whom I'd met that day. I shared the heaviness and worry I was feeling about Black women. We discussed how we face not just external sexism and racism, but how they worm their way into our psyche and do damage even when we're not actively experiencing them. We talked about our shared need to have a space with other Black women to talk about and work on ridding ourselves of that internalized oppression. Self-care wasn't enough; we wanted community care.

It took a year for us to actually have our first gathering. It was August 2016 when we met for the first time at my house. My dining room table overflowed with food as people showed up with bean salad, fried chicken, beef stew, fresh bread, cheese and crackers, wine, sparkling water, and pie. Nwamaka and I facilitated a conversation with more than twenty Black women exploring what freedom is. We talked about when we feel most free and how to build on that, what is blocking us, and what we can do about it. For most of us, it was the first time we'd been in a group of Black women that had come together with the express purpose of focusing on ourselves. More common in our experience was being in a group of Black women who were planning or laboring to achieve something for our communities or a cause we care about.

Initially, Nwamaka and I facilitated our gatherings. The conversations were powerful, heart-wrenching, and revelatory. Somewhere along the way, we dropped facilitation and just trusted that we'd talk about what we needed to. We open and close the circle with a prayer, poem, or reflection, and we've developed a culture of listening that allows us to be deeply present and vulnerable with one another. We go on field trips together—to the movies (our *Black Panther* viewing was lit!), performances, and festivals. We also have a group text where we ask for help, share affirmations, and check in with each other. Tammy reminds us, "I love y'all." Amber asks, "What thing will you do today to honor your relationship with yourself and your spirit?"

We are committed to caring for one another. We worry about one another. We celebrate one another.

Those Sunday mornings when we will gather at my house, I get up early to cook and clean (though usually Nino has already cleaned because he understands how important the gathering is for all of us, and he's more embarrassed than I am to have people in our home when it's a mess). I set seats in a circle in the living room. But I don't do much else because I know that whoever arrives first will help me get out plates and glasses, put on water for tea and coffee, and arrange food on the table.

Three hours later, we are cleaning up and embracing goodbye. When Nino returns with the kids, there are always leftovers for them and the kitchen is cleaner than it was to begin with. The idea of hosting can feel exhausting, but by the time everyone leaves, I am full and restored from our life-giving time together.

We can't fully know ourselves without other people. At the 2018 National Rural Assembly, legendary activist Ruby Sales said, "It is in community and in relationship with others that we locate a self that we can never find being isolated. It is in community and in relationship with each other that we come to know the consciousness and the spirit of god that is in each of us."[7] And we are closer to spirit, to whatever is divine in us and the universe, through our connections with other people. In this way, Black Women's Freedom Circle is my church.

What I feel at BWFC is an alchemy whereby we create more love and time and energy together than we hold individually. At our best, we don't function based on reciprocation. It's not about getting as much out of it as we put in. It's that our output is transformed into a wholly different material that's not possible to create alone, like we are spinning gold from straw or transforming paper cups into nebulae. It's only in an environment with others that this generative, multiplying power can be created.

Our joy becomes contagious. Our ability to love and comfort is expanded by others' grief, our own too-big-to-be-contained pain finds its freedom in others' witnessing of it. "Yes," they say, "feel it all. Don't be afraid to expand too wide or fall too far. We see you so you can't disappear." We ascend, we plummet, we break open, and we pull ourselves back together in the wellspring of the circle.

---

7. Daily Yonder, "A Dialogue with Reverend Jennifer Bailey and Ruby Sales," June 6, 2018, Vimeo video, https://vimeo.com/273731119.

Through these women, my understanding of care—care of myself and care of others—has become void of the binary framing of this or that, input and output. Suddenly, care of others *is* care of myself. Care of myself *is* care for others.

DISCOVERING WHO YOU ARE

This collective care creates an anchor from which I can practice self-care. To effectively care for myself—to understand what I need to support my own well-being—I have to be aware of myself. Self-awareness is critical for us individually, but it's also critical to having workable relationships. Shawna Sodersten, a marriage and family therapist,[8] says this: "Everybody's first job is to steward their own life experience. And that means discovering who you are, and all the things that bring you pleasure and joy, and feel aligned with you, and give you a sense of purpose."

Self-awareness is the bridge to healing our damage and trauma, and rewriting the stories that formed as a result. Shawna explains, we all have some "version of the story 'I am not safe' or 'I am not loved' or 'there's something wrong with me.' These beliefs shape what we pay attention to. Our selective attention shapes our perceptions, our perceptions shape our experience, our experience reinforces our beliefs, and round and round we go." Building self-awareness allows us to notice and reflect instead of just reacting. "Without this disruption, we create the same painful stories for ourselves and limit our capacity to give and receive connection."

---

8. Keeping it 100, she is my and Nino's therapist.

This part of us that notices is woken up and strengthened through mindfulness. If you've ever meditated, this is the part of you that notices you're thinking about how the bottom of your foot itches or trying to remember what you wanted to make for dinner, and it calls you back to the present.

I once met a physician—she was both a Western medical doctor and a practitioner of Chinese medicine—who told me that Western priorities around diet and exercise over mindfulness are backward. She said that, more than improving nutrition or working out, becoming more mindful would have a larger impact on one's health. I have no idea if that's accurate or what measure of impact she was referring to. But I do know that part of what capitalism does is create barriers to self-awareness. And of the three—exercise, nutrition, and mindfulness—mindfulness is the most accessible to the greatest number of people. Almost everyone, regardless of economic situation, physical ability, geography, and age, can pause for a moment and take a breath to check in with themselves. It doesn't require any special equipment, membership, location, or time of day. It might just be going from one job to another or in the shower or right before you get out of bed in the morning, but we can all access it.

Developing this self-awareness through mindfulness supports our ability to be in relationship with others because so often our reactions and the situations that prompt our reactive selves are, you know, because of other people.

Also key to being in relationship with other people is identifying and understanding our boundaries, which also requires self-awareness. I used to think of boundaries as a response—something I'd enact when people tried to impose upon me or demand something of me that I didn't want to give. That's not wrong, but it's not all of it.

Boundaries are what we want and don't want. Boundaries help us understand what is our stuff and what is not. Shawna explains, "One of the basic principles of boundaries work is to understand who is in charge of what. Who is responsible for what. So, we want to set up a world where each person is sovereign over themselves. So, what I'm in charge of includes my body, and my time, and my attention, and my trust, and my choices, and my behaviors, and my feelings. I'm in charge of all of that."

If self-awareness helps us notice when we're activated and running our old stories and patterns, boundaries help us take responsibility for all of that, and *not* take responsibility for other people's stuff when they're activated. I don't know about you, but sometimes I've confused the two. I have blamed others for my feelings of rejection or anxiety. I have also taken responsibility for other peoples' anger and disappointment.

In Shawna's work, she sees that there are some common places where people struggle with boundaries—saying and accepting no, and giving and receiving care.

Saying no is challenging for so many reasons. To start with, there are often consequences—others may not like our no and then we have to deal with their response. Saying no might cost us something. But part of our work is to evaluate the cost instead of just abdicating our agency.

For example, say you have a job in which the expectation is that everyone works twelve-hour days. If you say, "No, I am going to work eight-hour days," the consequence might be getting fired. Not having income is not a viable situation for most of us, so it doesn't seem like much of a choice. But it's important to recognize that it is—not because it suddenly gives you the power to change the situation you're in, but because it means you are clear about not wanting to be in it, and can make a plan for a future in which your situation is different. Instead of resigning yourself to staying and feeling pissed, depressed, or hopeless, you begin to understand your options and the various pros and cons of each one. That doesn't mean your boss isn't an asshole or is off the hook for creating unethical and unsustainable working conditions. Having agency doesn't mean it's your fault if you're in a bad situation. It just means you have the ability to recognize what it's costing you and work toward something that is your yes. This might be getting another job. Or maybe it's negotiating a raise at some point or organizing with your colleagues to demand more reasonable work hours.

To be sure, agency and choice exist on a spectrum. Part of what systemic oppression does is limit the choices and agency of the people who experience it. But it also works to convince us that we have *no* agency and *no* choice. As Alice Walker said, "The most common way people give up their power is by thinking they don't have any."

Saying no to people we like is also something many of us struggle with. As I've worked on my boundaries, I've found that I often don't even notice I'm saying yes because I don't recognize that there's a choice to be made. As a younger person, not wanting to hurt people's feelings, or make people uncomfortable, or fail to meet someone else's expectations meant I developed a practice of minimizing my own feelings and comfort. So much so that I often didn't even ask myself the question, Do I want this? Unsurprisingly, this was often in contexts with men and/or white and/or older people. While I was outspoken and would readily argue a perspective or interpretation in a class or work meeting, in my more personal relationships I tolerated a lot of bad sex, tedious interactions, flawed directions, and racist and sexist microaggressions.

Unlearning feeling responsible for someone's reaction to my "no" has been uncomfortable work. As a woman, I've been socialized to believe that what I want is secondary to what men want. The consent conversation, most recently spurred by the #MeToo movement, has opened up a much needed space for thinking about yeses and nos in the context of sexual intimacy. Given the prevalence of sexual assault and questionable sexual encounters, it's safe to say that many of us have had our boundaries crossed in ways that have made it hard to claim our agency or feel the edges of our boundaries.

I find inspiration, strength, and clarity from these words from Audre Lorde, "The speaking will get easier and easier. And you will find you have fallen in love with your own vision, which you may never have realized you had. And you will lose some friends and lovers, and realize you don't miss them. And new ones will find you and cherish you. And at last, you'll know with surpassing certainty that only one thing is more frightening than speaking your truth. And that is not speaking." While Lorde is talking about the danger of not speaking out against racism and sexism and homophobia and in service of freedom, I think it applies to our personal sense of boundaries and sovereignty too.

Saying no can be hard, and getting one can be hard too. When we get a no, it's normal to feel rejected, shamed, or misunderstood. But accepting the no is how we respect the no-er's autonomy and agency. If we recognize that the no is a boundary they're expressing, it gives us the opportunity to work through our own feelings instead of blaming them for making us feel bad. But when we respond by being passive-aggressive, defensive, pouting, or raging, we are violating their boundaries and not owning our stuff. That is obviously not how we want to be in our relationships.

One of the things I remind myself—and my loved ones remind me when I forget—is that my no isn't just a no, it is also a yes. When I'm clear enough to say no to what I don't want, then I have more room to say yes to what I do want. I can't have my true yeses without the nos. I want that for myself and the people I care about. I'm working on taking people's nos as information for me about who they are and trying to be pleased that they are listening to themselves.

The idea of asking for or accepting care is also an act of self-care many of us find challenging, and it is a recurring theme in almost every story in this book. The do-it-yourself-ness of the American Dream narrative has us refusing to ask for help, and often refusing to take it when offered because it's seen as shameful. Or, when we need help, we think of it as a burden on others. But the lone-wolf approach to life doesn't work for anyone because none of us is self-sufficient. Interdependence is part of who we are as people. We are fundamentally wired to need others.

"Love and belonging might seem like a convenience we can live without, but our biology is built to thirst for connection because it is linked to our most basic survival needs," explains Matthew D. Lieberman, a professor at UCLA who does research in social neuroscience.[9] In his book *Social: Why*

---

9. Matthew D. Lieberman, *Social: Why Our Brains Are Wired to Connect* (New York: Broadway Books, 2013), 43.

Our Brains Are Wired to Connect, he writes, "Our sociality is woven into a series of bets that evolution has laid down again and again throughout mammalian history. These bets come in the form of adaptations that are selected because they promote survival and reproduction."[10] Lieberman challenges our fundamental understanding of human needs, putting social connection that supports interdependence before even food, water, and shelter.[11]

If we don't ask for or accept help because of the independence we feel we must have, we don't offer it because of the scarcity we feel. One of the recurring sources of conflict between Nino and I is about time—who gets it and for what, whose activity is more necessary, whose time is more valuable, and what the tally is. While it's true that there are only so many hours in a day, that scarcity orientation has us hoarding time when we don't have to. When one of us stops for a moment and thinks, *I am going to make sure my partner gets the time they need and trust that I will get the same in return*, we ease into abundance. We feel better about what we are giving and what we are receiving. We both get what we need.

The closed off feeling of scarcity can make us stingy. One of the things we most miss out on by not having deep community is the abundance of support, resources, and care that exists when you've got many hearts and hands circling you. We can create more of what we all need when we are in community.

10. Lieberman, *Social*, 9.
11. Lieberman, *Social*, 48.

INTERDEPENDENCE OUTSIDE COUPLEDOM

Although Nino and I can sometimes be more generous with each other when it comes to time or other needs we have, sometimes the solution is that we need to count on more people. And that means pushing against our ideas about being in a couple and what marriage is for.

According to the American Dream ideal, your relationship with a spouse or romantic partner is meant to be the most important one you have. The insular nuclear family, around which our personal life is supposed to orbit, is built from matrimony. It's a reinforcing of the independent individual, recast as the independent couple. Spouses are meant to fulfill a wide range of roles in our lives—lover, best friend, caretaker, housemate, confidant, coparent, cofinance and household manager, activity and travel buddy. That is an impossibly high bar for two people to meet for each other. I'm sure there are some (no doubt, smug) couples who do a good job at all of those things. But those relationships, which meet a standard modeled in an infinite number of fairy tales, movies, and TV shows, are absolute anomalies.

It's not that couples can't be many things to and for each other, but excelling at them all is unlikely. Nino and I have lived together for more than fifteen years and I'm still a terrible housemate. We each have deep passions that the other doesn't share. We have other people with whom we share interests, who we rely on for counsel, and who we travel with. But I still feel the inward orientation our lives take. It's partly because that's how we started out—there are some things that would be hard to unravel from coupledom, like finances and parenting—and it's also what we're used to.

We tend to isolate some when we fall in love. That isolation means that people in couples often bear the brunt of each other's stress and anger and pain. This dynamic is especially true for straight couples. Because of the socialization men get, they are less likely than women to develop emotionally intimate relationships outside their romantic/sexual relationships. This means that their female partners are doing a tremendous amount of emotional labor that isn't reciprocated. And women, well, we are socialized toward caretaking and feeling rewarded when our male partners (and male friends) confide in and lean on us. But, over time, the weight of that can be too much for a relationship. And it doesn't allow us to benefit from the wisdom of others or practice asking for and accepting support.

When men lose their female partners because of death or divorce, they are often set adrift. Whereas, anecdotally, women who lose male partners seem to thrive. Among the sixty-five-plus-and-dating set, "more older women are rejecting the downsides of the live-in relationship: the co-dependence, the daily tension within close quarters and the sacrifices made keeping a home, caregiving and doing the emotional legwork to keep their unions humming."[12]

Too, those who don't get coupled up, or do so later in life, are often a bit abandoned by their friends who pair off. Or they are in groups of other singles with no blueprint for how to manage some of the things we expect a spouse or partner to be part of—death of a parent, care when we get sick,

---

12. Zosia Bielski, "The New Reality of Dating over 65: Men Want to Live Together; Women Don't," *The Globe and the Mail*, November 30, 2019, https://www.theglobeandmail.com/life/relationships/article-women-older-than-65-dont-want-to-live-with-their-partners/.

celebrating our accomplishments, taking vacations, coming to the doctor with us or driving us home from the hospital, staging an intervention when we struggle with addiction. But there is no reason our friends can't do these things for us. And for those of us with partners, there's no reason we can't spread some of the expectations we have of our partners around to other people. Let's dismantle the primacy of the conventional romantic couple for the benefit of all of us.

SHIFTS IN ATTENTION THAT HAPPEN WHEN YOU MAKE SOMEONE FAMILY

I knew I loved Mariah when I got an email she sent to a handful of parents asking if we knew of any oceanographers of color. My daughter Stella was in Mariah's kindergarten and first-grade classes and they were beginning their unit on oceans. As the end of first grade drew closer, I felt a growing sense of loss. We'd see Mariah at school, but not as regularly as we did during the years she was Stella's teacher. So, one day after school, I gathered my courage and asked her if she would be Stella's auntie and my friend. She immediately smiled her signature Mariah smile and said yes. I felt a deep sense of relief and joy that this amazing, brilliant person would not only continue to be part of our lives, but be family.

Mariah and I have a lot in common. We were both raised by our white mothers and had Jamaican fathers. Our dads are dead and our relationships with our mothers are not without complication. We've bonded over being mixed-race Black women, being raised by white women, our relationship with Jamaica, art, politics, relationships, food, and any number of other things. We've collaborated on various projects and she's a go-to person for so much of the work I do. Mariah has helped me love, appreciate, understand, and participate in art in new ways. She has advanced my skills as a facilitator and curator of spaces in which others can learn and grow. Her laugh is spectacular and contagious—and it's not just that she makes me laugh when she laughs, but my laugh has morphed to sound more like hers.

Mariah was twelve when she was diagnosed with type 1 diabetes. She experienced a lot of fear around her diagnosis. "I mean, diabetes has 'die' in it, you know?" She had to develop an awareness of her body and a practice of self-care that most young people—or adults, for that matter—don't. "You live with this impending doom because your whole situation is about keeping your body alive moment to moment. At any moment you could have low blood sugar, just because you forgot to eat a snack or you took too much insulin and then you walked an extra mile or something happens out of the blue that you can't account for."

Most children with diabetes have a parent who is helping them manage their condition. But Mariah, who was raised by her mother, has a sister with special needs, so she took on the bulk of her care herself. I've had glimpses into what that care looks like. When we spend time together, Mariah periodically takes out her insulin pump to check her insulin or blood sugar. When we travel together, she has to worry about airport security because she almost always gets questions about her pump, which she wears under her clothes and is attached to a catheter that delivers insulin into her bloodstream. But I know that barely touches the surface of what she is managing on an hourly basis. "Your emotional mind is totally wrapped in survival mode constantly. So, it's like having two brains.

One brain is full-on survival and the other brain is trying to participate in the world."

The specificity of the experience has created an opportunity for diabetics to be in community starting from a young age. Mariah started going to Bearskin Meadow Camp when she was thirteen. There, kids who have diabetes learn to take care of their body, developing the kind of self-sufficiency necessary for them to manage their condition. But they also learn to become reliant on others. When Mariah arrived a year after she'd been managing diabetes on her own, it was hard for her to trust others with her care. "I was in such panic that I would take sugar cubes and hide them in my clothing and under my bed, which you're not supposed to do because of bears. I wanted to make sure that at any moment I could have them, because I didn't know if anyone would understand how I looked when my blood sugar was low."

But the diabetes camp knows what it's doing. The culture is like wilderness camp with swimming and theater and day hikes, plus morning insulin lines before breakfast and doctors checking on you in the middle of the night. It's a place where diabetes is totally normalized—no one looks at you when you whip out your pump or prick your finger to check your blood sugar. All the attention you pay to eating, moving, hydration, stress, and any number of other things that can affect you isn't seen as obsessive or tedious.

As important, Mariah saw people of all ages—kids attending camp and counselors in their sixties—thriving, happy, and healthy living with diabetes. It was the place that made her realize that she was going to be okay.

A few years ago, Mariah was hospitalized for the first time in her life for an insulin reaction. It rocked her world emotionally because she took great pride in her independent management of her condition. Like me, like so many of us, she was reluctant to ask for help and support. Part of it is the sense of agency that comes from being able to take care of yourself, especially when you have a chronic illness and don't want to be hindered by the availability (or lack thereof) of others. At the same time, we people need one another.

Since then, I've learned more about how much of Mariah's time, mental energy, income, and other resources are directed at managing her diabetes. But it wasn't until a recent conversation about the apocalypse (an increasingly common topic of discussion for me) that I began to realize how little I knew and how significant a resource drain it is. We were talking about how to acquire a steady supply of insulin if there was a shortage (which there may be in the next decade or so) or there was no power (insulin needs to be kept cool). The next morning, I went down an internet rabbit hole reading up on insulin. Not only does it have to be kept refrigerated, but it has a short shelf life. Unlike most common drugs, which can last years and only lose effectiveness past their prime, insulin can go bad and potentially harm you. There's no plant-based alternative for insulin or a temporary fix if you run out. I read the actual process for creating it (from pig pancreases), which is complicated, precise, and requires equipment and chemicals that are not easy to acquire (you know, like a pharmaceutical lab). I started reading about the biohacker start-ups that want to make insulin creation as easy as home brewing beer. It all made me a little panicky. And then, I thought, *Never mind the apocalypse, I need to be better prepared to care for Mariah now.*

Over the years, she has occasionally texted me because her blood sugar got really low and she wanted me to check in on her to make sure she hadn't slipped into a coma. This was progress from the days of wanting to handle it all herself, but I wanted to be better prepared. What should I tell an EMT or emergency room doctor if she had a medical emergency? What kind of first aid might I have to do on her? Where are her drugs, juice boxes, and needles? How would I get into her house in an emergency? Who would I need to call if something happened to her?

I had some trepidation about bringing all of this up with her. What if this was getting all up in her business in ways that were nosy and not helpful? What if I was making a bunch of assumptions that were offensive in some way? Maybe she had done this with other close friends and didn't need me to insert myself. But I thought about how hard it is for people to ask for help in a moment of need. How many of us ask for people to prepare to help us when the need isn't actually present? So, I brought it all up with her and asked if we could make a date to sit down so she could tell me all of these things, plus whatever else she thought I should know. She enthusiastically agreed and said that no one had ever asked. I know it's not because her other friends are jerks and I'm so caring and thoughtful. I think it's because the expectation we grow up with is that we will have a long-term partner whose job it is to hold important information and take care of us. We don't have a public practice of doing that job outside of marriage.

So, we made a date to meet and talk. She created a document that she gave to me and a few other friends. She took me through everything—her insurance info, doctors' contact numbers, which insulin pump she uses, allergies, emergency contacts—all of it. I put an app on my phone that alerts me if Mariah's blood sugar gets dangerously low. I used to put my phone on airplane mode when I went to sleep, but now it stays on. I check it almost every night to make sure it's working. If I travel somewhere where I don't have phone service, I let her know in advance.

These are small adjustments, but they are the kinds of little shifts in attention that happen when you make someone family. This new attention helps me see a little more into her experience, and while I will never fully see it or understand what it's like, I can work to keep that window open more often and make it bigger.

THREE

Love Is Abundant and Every Relationship Is Unique

The Queering of Friendship

i want a world where when people ask if we are seeing anyone we can list the names of all our best friends and no one will bat an eyelid. i want monuments and holidays and certificates and ceremonies to commemorate friendship.[1]

—ALOK VAID-MENON

M Y CONVERSATION WITH Mariah had me thinking about the other people I'm close to—single and not—and wondering what I should ask them about medical conditions and caring for them in emergencies. I've taken care of friends' pets and have more information on the medical needs, food requirements, and emergency contact numbers of the pets than I do on my friends. More broadly, what are the other ways in which we could be caring for one another? What spaces in our lives could we open up to one another?

---

1. Alok Vaid-Menon, "Friendship Is Romance," *Alok* (blog), February 15, 2017, https://www.alokvmenon.com/blog/2017/2/15/friendship-is -romance.

What parameters have been set for us by convention that are keeping us out of one another's business?

There is a line to cross toward more intimacy and interdependence when we put aside the modern conventions of friendship and get up in one another's business. On the other side is not a single alternative or even just a handful of options. There is a whole spectrum of possible relationships. I can look at each of my friendships as singular pairings with its own culture, standard of operating, behavioral norms and communication approach, expectations and commitments. The culture of a friendship is something we can make up if we take the opportunity to talk about what we want it to be. That infinite possibility is freeing.

The space on the other side of that line may be unconventional for cishet[2] people, but among many of my queer[3] friends and family, I see a different norm that points me forward. Queer people have long articulated and practiced a wider spectrum of relationships than cishet people. The idea of platonic boyfriends/girlfriends/partners and "Boston marriages" (a nineteenth-century phrase describing two women who shared a life and lived together without the support of a man) has been around for a while. Back in the day, sometimes these relationships were actually sexual relationships between folks who couldn't be out as gay because it was illegal, socially

---

2. *Cishet* is short for *cisgender*—someone who identifies as the gender they were assigned at birth—and *heterosexual*.

3. I'm using *queer* in the broadest sense here. It's the LGBT folks, but also people who are nonbinary, gender nonconforming, aromantic, and asexual. If any of this terminology is new to you, the internet is your teacher. Just avoid the religious right, the haters, and the incels in your research.

unacceptable, and dangerous. But sometimes they were intimate nonsexual friendships.

A more modern umbrella term for these relationships is
queerplatonic. The word was coined, defined, and redefined
by asexual and aromantic people[4] to describe a relationship
that is not romantic, but emotionally closer than what we
generally think of as friendship. The "queer" part is not about
sexuality, but about the queering of our ideas about what relationships look like. As writer and activist Shon Faye puts
it, "Queer is about removing labels and replacing them with a
question. It is a side eye and a challenge back to mainstream
society and politics. It says, 'I don't know the answer, but
why are you asking the question?'"[5] Queering relationships is
rejecting the restraints of convention, but it's also liberatory
truth-finding. It allows us to look at a relationship (and so
many other things) stripped of preconceptions and ask, *What
is this really? What are the components? What is happening inside
of it?* Anyone of any sexual orientation, gender, or other relationships status can be in a queerplatonic relationship.

Having more language and examples that articulate a way
to be in relationship with others outside conventional understanding is affirming because I have, and want more, relationships like that. Even though I'm not aromantic or asexual, the
paths people with those identities are forging to be wholly

---

4. To be clear, there is no agreed-upon definition. A Genealogy of
Queerplatonic (a potential rabbit hole) is helpful and can be found at
https://theacetheist.wordpress.com/2019/03/09/a-genealogy-of-queer
-platonic/.

5. Shon Faye, "What Does It Mean to Be Queer?" March 13, 2016,
YouTube video, https://www.youtube.com/watch?v=RDO2-sNF2s4.

who they are makes room for the rest of us too. People are living into identities that aren't accepted or even recognized by society at large. Their insistence on self-definition creates space for all of us to be more self-determined.

Let me be very clear about a few things right now, though. There is a lot of writing about queerness, queering, and queer theory. I have read, heard, and been schooled by loved ones on some of it. But I am not an expert on queerness. If you aren't either, I invite you to join me in the lifelong role of student. In writing about this, I very much want to stay in my lane. As a cishet person, that lane is primarily about interrogating homophobia, heterosexism, relationship hierarchy, and the binary norming of gender, sexuality, and identity to do my part dismantling systems that uphold all of that, including the ways in which I personally uphold them. But it's not just about increasing the absence of oppression. It's also about practicing something else in its place. It's about increasing liberation.

BUT! This is not about appropriating or gentrifying queerness. I don't get to wrap a rainbow around my relationships while holding tightly to the benefits of being a cishet person, and not show up for queer people. Straight and/or cisgender folks don't get to be the people who benefit most from the work queer people do to make themselves more free. I have a responsibility to listen, to care for, to defend, to protect. I'm often doing it because I know it's the right thing to do and it aligns with my values and beliefs. But more and more, I'm doing it because I see clearly that my freedom is tied to queer people's freedom.

I'm trying to step outside the narrow list of possibilities that we've been given. Part of this means squashing the relationships hierarchy that says a monogamous romantic/ sexual relationship is infinitely more important than the other relationships in our lives. For me, that doesn't mean diminishing my marriage, but elevating other relationships.

So often we believe that following the traditions we know is an easy path because there are fewer decisions to make and there's less friction with other people's expectations and society's rules of acceptance. We buy into the idea that tradition is better in some way—a thing to uphold and safekeep or American Dreamism's promised path to happiness. We may choose a little bit of unconvention—living on a houseboat, freelance podcasting, becoming a beekeeper. But so many of us end up in relationships, locations, jobs, routines, etc., because it was the only option we saw or we were afraid of not doing the "right" thing. But there's no ease here. The dissatisfaction, depression, and sense of loss people feel in spaces or norms that don't work for them can be devastating. And when we don't see or encounter other possibilities, it can take such a long time for us to figure out that we want something else. It's one thing to feel that something else is not really possible. In our society, systems create very real constraints for people who have limited money or are women, queer, or have a disability, for example. But we also put constraints on ourselves, we live inside them, we hold on to them hoping for the promise we think "normal" holds.

A BEAUTIFUL AND BELLIGERENT TRADITION

"I think of my family as a queer family even when it's full of straight people. This is an unconventional approach to family," Gabi, who is queer, transgender, and genderqueer,[6] told me, reflecting on the idea that "queering" is about bucking convention—not just for its own sake, but because it's what actually works. They told me, "I love the defiance of the bumper sticker 'Not gay as in happy but queer as in fuck you.'"

Gabi is "mixed race, white-presenting, Mexican American, and (at least) fifth-generation Californian" on both sides of their biological family. Their earliest memories are being at family gatherings, looking around the room and thinking, "These aren't my people. I don't belong here, but I need to wait it out, and then my people will come and get me." This feeling of being out of place and not belonging was compounded by not having a sense of what something better looked like. But they did have an idea of what it would feel like to be at home with people, to be loved and love them, and they managed to create that for themselves.

When Gabi was in middle school, their parents' best friend was a woman called Gwen. "She was amazing. She was this supercrotchety, high fem, old-school lesbian. She was a thrift store dressing person, and had a dog, and drove a Jeep, and chain-smoked, and she had no filter." Gabi's

---

6. "Genderqueer: An identity commonly used by people who do not identify or express their gender within the gender binary. Those who identify as genderqueer may identify as neither male nor female, may see themselves as outside of or in between the binary gender boxes, or may simply feel restricted by gender labels. Many genderqueer people are cisgender and identify with it as an aesthetic. Not everyone who identifies as genderqueer identifies as trans or nonbinary." —https://www.transstudent.org/definitions

parents didn't really have any other friends, so Gwen's friends became their friends and, by extension, Gabi's aunts, uncles, and cousins.

When Gabi was in their early twenties, Gwen was diagnosed with terminal cancer. ("The doctor said, 'I think you've got three to six months,' and she looked right back at the doctor and said, 'I don't think it'll take that long.' She died twenty-three days later.") People came to see her to give her love and say good-bye. One of those people was an ex-girlfriend called Deborah. "She was just the coolest fucking person I'd ever met. She kind of reminded me of George Carlin in her delivery of everything she said. She was an artist—a painter—living in New York." After Gwen's memorial, Gabi and Deborah stayed in touch, sometimes sending each other sketches in the mail. They'd visit each other when Gabi was in New York or Deborah was in the Bay Area, where Gabi lives.

On one visit, Deborah was behaving strangely, like she wanted to say something but wasn't quite ready to or didn't know how. Gabi's fear was that she was dying. After Deborah left, Gabi got an email from her: "Sorry, it's weird what I was trying to ask, but can I put you down as my power of attorney? Can we talk about advanced health-care directives?" Deborah's other friends were either her age, older, or "already dead" and she didn't want her estate going to her biological family because she wasn't close to them. Gabi of course said yes.

In reflecting on their relationships, Gabi said, "I don't even know what the trajectory of the geometry of something like that is. My parents' best friend when I was in middle school, who I came to think of as my godmother, even though she wasn't, her girlfriend from the '70s, then buddy, became one of my cranky hangout and beer buddies, and now we're like family. It makes no sense, but I love it."

That unknowable geometry is how Gabi met Alexis as well. Alexis was the partner of Gabi's closest friend, Anna. Gabi and Alexis had only met a few times before Anna first attempted suicide. After her second attempt, which she died from, they met in person. "It was like this weird zero to sixty disaster-driven closeness." At some point, their friendship became about what they shared in addition to loving and losing the same person. Now, years later, the two remain close. They have their own running private jokes and, after months of grieving together in person and over texts, they developed a deep sense of comfort with each other. They sometimes "get together and ignore each other"—like being in a room together, each reading their own book.

"It's strange to look at him and know that the reason that he and I are close is because she's no longer here, and what that's done to both of us. But I would commit felonies for this man at this point. We're in it."

Gabi is someone who has long felt most comfortable outside what is given to, or expected of, them. They told me, "I use 'queer' to describe most aspects of my identity because apart from the definition as 'not-straight,' I see it as meaning odd and not fitting easily with where I came from. I love queerness so much as a beautiful and belligerent tradition of people whose sense of love and beauty and justice and art and adventure and family is too expansive for the examples that were set for us. But rather than keep quiet, we insist on something truer for ourselves."

PLATONIC PARTNERS AND PLUS-ONES

"In the Harpy House, we don't have rules," Jade told me. "When there's a problem, we have a conversation. The reason people have 'house rules' is to avoid conflict, but you're not going to avoid conflict. The conflict is going to happen. So, how are you going to deal with it when it comes up?"

Jade is my sister-in-love, Nino's sister, and an extraordinary aunt to our kids. Harpy House, where she lives, is an old Victorian with faded Buddhist prayer flags at the entrance and mannequin hands attached to the front stairs, like they are offering to help your ascent.

"When someone has a problem, everyone brings it up right away. People figure out pretty fast when they're introduced to the community, whether or not that works for them."

Jade sits at the center of this household with a set of skills she learned from growing up at Finegold, an intentional community in rural California situated in the Sierra Nevada foothills.

"There was an old guard that had invested their lives into creating this community that was meant to be creative and cooperative—an everyone-puts-in, everyone-gets-out kind of community. When I came along—I was born in 1983—a lot of that energy had started to die off." The community mostly drifted apart when she was in her teens, but there remain deep, lasting connections among the people who were part of it. "In any city in the United States, and probably anywhere in the world, I can make a few phone calls and find someone that's connected to Finegold somehow. They would be like, 'You're cool, you're with Finegold. You can sleep on my couch or whatever.'"

Harpy House became what it is largely because of Jade. In 2014 she moved into what was then a house with an assortment of people renting rooms. They would come out to use the bathroom or kitchen, but otherwise stayed in their own rooms, while common spaces were deserted. "There was a layer of dust over everything and a little path to the kitchen and to the fridge and that's it. First, I scrubbed everything. Once everything was clean, I did what my mom taught me how to do—you make a pot of soup. Then all the hungry little people will come out of their rooms. And they're like, 'The house is really clean and there's soup!' Then they hang out and get to know each other."

Today, there are five white queer cis and transgender people in their twenties and thirties living in Harpy House, along with several dogs, cats, rabbits, and ducks. Jade and her housemates are chosen family to one another and that sense of family extends to former housemates, current partners, and a handful of others who consider Harpy House a second home.

"It took being at Harpy House, where it was stable and calm and there are supportive people around me, for me to realize that the people I consider family are not the people who I see all the time and have lots of fun times with," Jade told me. "It's the people who check in on me when they haven't heard from me for a few days, or remember what's going on with me—'Oh, I know you had that stressful thing,' or 'I brought you tacos unexpectedly,' or 'Oh, I heard you weren't feeling well physically, so I'm gonna come and help you do your laundry.'"

In Harpy House, there's an extra bedroom they don't rent out anymore because it's hot in the summer, has no storage, and picks up "party noise" from the neighbors. But it's become a space for people in housing transitions, people who need to detox from drugs, or people recovering from surgery. When one of their housemates had surgery, her caretakers stayed in that room so they could give her medication and switch out her ice packs in the middle of the night.

When Noah, who is a freelance sign language interpreter, moved into Harpy House, he and Jade became friends over coffee in the mornings. "The weather's nice, we sit outside, and—Oh! It's three o'clock in the afternoon," Jade explained, and Noah chimed in. "Whoever got up first would make the coffee and then whoever was still asleep was like, oh, the grinder's starting, I'd better get up."

"That was how it started," Jade continued. "And it just became an unspoken thing that we have coffee together and we talk about everything. I was just like, oh my god, it's so nice that you shared this whole problem that you're having with me and then took a breath and then let me talk about what's going on with me."

Noah grew up in an intentional community as well, though his was organized around religion. It instilled in him an understanding of family that was much broader than the nuclear one. "My experience was that I had eighteen siblings and fifty parents. As kids, we had work days. We would just play together in an old chicken coop that had been renovated and then we would work on teams. Most of it was really gendered, so I spent a lot more time in the kitchen and the sewing teams than I spent doing electrical or outdoors work because I was a little girl." (Noah is a transgender man and was assigned female at birth.)

Jade and Noah are, as Jade said, "platonic partners." Noah often comes to our family gatherings like Christmas and birthday parties. They have an ongoing conversation about becoming coparents.

They both date and have romantic-sexual relationships with other people, but they play a role for each other that is outside the convention of friendship.

Deanna Zandt has a similar relationship. "It started out as a joke that we would clean out each other's nightstands before the other's mother got there if something happened to us," Deanna told me as we laughed thinking about the journals, sex toys, and other things one might keep next to one's bed. Then she and her friend Cynthia became each other's plus-ones at weddings and parties, and they started talking about retiring together. And then the partner of one of Cynthia's friends died very suddenly.

Cynthia began worrying about what would happen to her if she died alone in her apartment. Deanna suggested they start texting each other every morning to make sure the other was okay. "It was an intentional thing. Then we shared each other's important phone numbers, who has a set of keys nearby, all that stuff. We text every single day now. We haven't missed a day in years. That has created this scaffolding for other deeper-based touching than I normally would with some of my other friends." Cynthia and Deanna have created a partnership that has much of the safety, commitment, emotional support, and intimacy of marriage without the sex. Deanna's mom even treats Cynthia like a daughter-in-law. They both date, but neither wants children or a conventional marriage.

Deanna grew up in a traditional semirural community. But her next-door neighbor Louise was anything but traditional.

"Louise was Irish Catholic and she married a Jewish man twenty years older than her, which for my small town was probably pretty scandalous. She said people would ask her if she converted and she would tell people that she was Jewish by injection."

Louise's husband died when she was in her early sixties. After her husband died, she continued her unconventional life. She and her best friend, Betty, traveled to Ireland and Germany. They'd go stay in the Adirondacks every year. She brought Betty to events like graduations or annual picnics. As a result, Deanna, whose family moved next door to Louise the year before Deanna was born, grew up with this idea that "When you get old, someone dies, and then you hang out with your friends." Louise became very close to Deanna's family, joining the family much like the rotation of cousins and others who would sometimes live in Deanna's house.

Deanna's parents are also very independent, so when she started to encounter people who centered their romantic relationships at the expense of other relationships, it didn't make much sense to her.

Deanna celebrated her fortieth birthday by marrying her community of friends.[7] She rented a rooftop, hired caterers and photographers, and held a ceremony. That community included a group of people who she became close to in the aftermath of September 11, 2001. The month prior, she'd moved to New York's Lower East Side and a friend told her about the bar around the corner. ("It was lovely. It was just this nice neighborhood bar.") On September 12, in a mental and emotional fog and horror, many people from the

7. Courtney Martin, "For Her 40th Birthday, This Woman 'Married' Her Community," *Washington Post*, September 14, 2016, https://www.washingtonpost.com/news/soloish/wp/2016/09/14/for-her-40th-birthday-this-woman-married-her-community/.

neighborhood ended up at the bar. "We were all just there like, What the fuck? What is any of this?"

Being together—to process, to avoid processing—was solidifying for the group of about a dozen people who regularly gathered at the bar following "the disaster," as they called it. They started thinking of the bar as their living room. The tiny apartments they all occupied did not lend themselves to group hangouts, so they'd go to the bar "to watch TV and order food and not be alone."

The experience of coming together around 9/11, sharing their "Where were you?" stories (which included the man who only survived because he was too hungover to go to work that day when his whole office died), and knowing one another's stories so they didn't have to keep telling them, built bonds they shared uniquely with one another.

Deanna remembers going to her hometown for the holidays and being asked repeatedly to share her 9/11 story. With people who hadn't been through it with her, it felt more like voyeurism than helpful processing. It didn't feel good to talk about it. Returning to her group at the bar felt like going home, even if that home was full of shared trauma.

The group maintained its solidity for more than five years, until people began moving away, splitting off into couples (several members of the group married each other), and experiencing the shifts we often do as we transition from our twenties to our thirties. But Deanna remains close with many of those people, and it's where her relationship with Cynthia formed and solidified.

Deanna, who practices ethical nonmonogamy in her romantic-sexual relationships, likes the idea of having less hierarchy in her relationships. Unlike conventional arrangements, it's her relationship with Cynthia that sits at the top of her relationship hierarchy. "I want other people to know that this is one of the most important people to me in my life and they should respect her and treat her not just as a friend of mine but as someone that is like a partner to me."

RELATIONSHIP ANARCHY

When I was a preteen, several of the books I loved featured passionate but seemingly chaste female friendships bound in sisterhood during a ceremonial mingling of blood. The characters would prick or cut a finger and press them together, marking their pledge to each other as blood sisters.

I love this practice, as unsanitary as it is, because it's a commitment ritual for friendship that is otherwise absent in our culture. Commitment to another individual happens implicitly through biology and explicitly through marriage and adoption. But friendship, particularly adult friendship, has no such vow.

It's not that we don't experience commitment inside our friendships. But we don't often declare it. Through support and help, through engagement and participation, we extend our time and energy to people we are committed to. But the degree to which we are committed bumps up against that lack of clarity when we want a friendship to hold significance in our lives that looks closer to what our culture expects from romantic love. I wonder what we are missing out on by not clarifying the expectations and boundaries of our friendships and our hopes for those relationships.

What would it look like if we had more models for articulating our commitment to our friendships? Not just that we are committed, but what that commitment looks like, what they can expect from us and us from them. What spaces for safety and intimacy and care would that open up for us? Would we have more support when we were sick or grieving, or facing hardships like losing a job or a home? Would we have more room in our lives to take risks and follow dreams if we were making those decisions inside committed friendships?

Commitment like that requires some communication around expectations. While we can presume that our romantic-sexual relationships will include conversations to negotiate and work toward shared understanding, we expect a kind of effortlessness when it comes to friendships. This can prevent them from being as deep as they might be.

Teddy and I are, in many ways, an odd match. He is a single, straight, white dad who grew up in the suburbs of Chicago in a fairly conventional nuclear family. He works for a giant tech firm, doing something that I don't really understand. He's an introvert, I am not. He ruminates, I think out loud.

We met at an introductory dinner for an advisory board we both sat on. I arrived late and the only available seat was across from him. I'd read everyone's bios and there was nothing about his that I found interesting. But shortly after sitting down, I was pulled in. He wasn't charismatic—I don't know that he'd said much of anything, but I felt drawn to him. If I believed in past lives, I'd assume we'd been each other's family. The next time we saw each other, I just behaved as if our close relationship was a foregone conclusion. I'd claimed him as one of my people.

We practiced a kind of reckless vulnerability and honesty with our unproven but mutual trust. It's like we met and immediately became high-flying trapeze partners. He made a commitment to our friendship early on when I expressed apprehension about all the leaps of faith. That commitment from him, reciprocated by me, gave us room to mess up even though we each worried about disappointing the other. But we approach each other with the benefit of the doubt and a spirit of inquiry. The care and solidity with which we've handled the great emotional risk we entrusted each other with established not just safety and trust but a practice of talking about the things that make us feel most vulnerable and embarrassed or unsure.

"There's the really deep, mature emotional relationship and support that I look to our friendship for," he told me. "It's literally the support, but also the *model* of that support—how we are mature, grown-ass adults about it. I get actual support, and a model in the dynamic you and I have. The second part is every bit as valuable as the first."

We also model personal growth for each other. We inspire each other toward our best selves but can share our flaws with each other. "It's easy to be vulnerable around you," he told me, "because you're also vulnerable in the sense of, like, 'I'm just learning here, I'm just growing.' I think that stance we're able to have with each other takes away so much baggage that I have in other relationships."

We are among each other's closest confidants and have supported each other through a lot of hardness. We don't go more than a couple of days without texting or talking on the phone. I am still sometimes confounded by how it's worked out and ultimately it reminds me that love can look like lots of things.

Our relationship has confounded other people too, particularly its emotional intimacy. And I get it. The expectation that straight men and women can't be that close without having sex (or wanting to have sex) is a pretty intransigent one. Andie Nordgren's "The short instructional manifesto for relationship anarchy" is an exhilarating pushback to this and other limiting relationship frames.[8] The manifesto speaks to what it might look like for us to prioritize and honor our friendships in a way that allows for a more expansive understanding of what friendship is. Nordgren writes that "relationship anarchy questions the idea that love is a limited resource that can only be real if restricted to a couple."

The first tenet of the manifesto is "Love is abundant, and every relationship is unique." It questions a culture that tells us we have limited love to give, and that the learned parameters of romantic-sexual love and friendship are our only options when it comes to the relationships we build with others. adrienne maree brown warns that "We're all going to die if we keep loving this way, die from isolation, loneliness, depression, abandoning each other to oppression, from lack of touch, from forgetting we are precious."[9] This first tenet invites us to open up and feel our way toward each relationship's distinct landscape.

But stepping outside these constructs is, like any process of undoing socialization, hard. We have to be vigilant. That is easier to do when you know what you're aspiring to. Another

---

8. Andie Nordgren, "The short instructional manifesto for relationship anarchy," The Anarchist Library, July 14, 2012, https://theanarchist library.org/library/andie-nordgren-the-short-instructional-manifesto -for-relationship-anarchy. In addition to Nordgren's piece, I highly recommend reading up on relationship anarchy in general.

9. adrienne maree brown, *Pleasure Activism: The Politics of Feeling Good* (Edinburgh: AK Press, 2019), 60.

tenet of the manifesto is "Find your core set of relationship values." Nordgren helps us figure that out by asking, "How do you wish to be treated by others? What are your basic boundaries and expectations in all relationships? What kind of people would you like to spend your life with, and how would you like your relationships to work?" This is where that self-awareness work comes in handy.

Perhaps part of our challenge in thinking expansively about our friendships is that we're limited by the word *friend*. Like *community*, the word *friend* has come to be so broad as to have lost meaning. We can have thousands of "friends" on social media, including people we have never met and make no effort to know. *Friend* can describe a work acquaintance whose personal life you know nothing about or a close intimate with whom you share history and your realest self. There are beautiful words in languages other than English that get at some of the richness and variety of friendship, like the Gaelic phrase *anam cara*, which literally translates as "soul friend"; or the Aramaic *havruta*, which means "friend" and, depending on your brand of Judaism, can mean a person with whom you study the Torah or someone with whom you engage in self-education; or the Japanese *nakama*, which can mean "buddy" or "people who you can trust in all things."[10] And then there is the Black American practice of applying familial words to friends who are like family, like *auntie* or *brother*. Knowing that there are other words supports my ability to see the possibilities that were previously obscured to me even if I never use them.

---

10. From Mari Noguchi, a Japanese-language cataloger, librarian, and native speaker of Japanese.

FRIENDSHIP PERMACULTURE

When the regular demands of life sap our strategic thinking capacity, we can be less thoughtful about decisions we make about anything, including our relationships. I know that for me, the constant mild overwhelm means sometimes I'm flaky with friendships or I don't take time to be thoughtful about who I'm prioritizing.

Lawrence Barriner II, a communications strategist, applied to his friendships a system of zones inspired by permaculture, a system of design principles that helps farmers and gardeners be efficient with their resources and energy.[11] Zone 1 holds those he is closest to. "These are people that I structure my life and time around."[12] Zone 5 is people he doesn't know exist. I followed up with Lawrence a little over a year after he wrote about friend zones to ask him how it was going. While there are pieces of it that he hasn't figured out, the most successful part has been around Zone 1: "This structure is magical," he wrote; "it allows me to really feel good about making time and space to connect with folks who i know deeply and who know me deeply. after knowing someone for years and years, a one hour conversation is worth like 50 hours of one-off conversations. they can be so healing and rejuvenating and they often help me remember i am loved, i love, and remind me what matters."[13]

---

11. Lawrence Barriner II, "Why I'm Putting EVERYONE in the Friend Zone," *Medium*, December 1, 2017, https://medium.com/@lq b2/planning-out-my-friend-ecosystem-95175246458d.

12. Barriner, "Why I'm Putting EVERYONE."

13. Lawrence Barriner II, "Friend Zones Update: How It's Going," *lgb2writes* (blog), February 19, 2019, http://lqb2.co/blog///2019/02/19 /friend-zone-update/.

After reading Barriner's original piece, I made a list of the people I consider my Zone 1 equivalents. I put this list on a bright pink sticky note on the wall in front of my desk. Amid the quotes, drawings, and poems is a list of about sixteen people I love dearly, not including the people I live with. I see it almost every day and it keeps them from receding too far from the top of my mind.

The list also kind of makes me feel like an asshole. Who needs to keep a list of the people they love to remember to stay in touch with them? But apparently I do. And I'd rather feel like an asshole than behave like one. It reminds me to reach out—to say I love you, to ask how they're doing, to make a plan to meet up. It reminds me to tell Aisha I'm thinking about her or schedule a date with Liz or find out when Dana is back in town so we can cowork together.

While part of what I'm working toward is flattening the relationship hierarchy, I'm also clear that my friendships are part of what keep my marriage working. I get a range of love, affirmation, attention, inspiration, perspective, and engagement that isn't dependent on my husband or the state of our relationship. My husband, as wonderful as he is, does not have much to offer me when it comes to some things that are important to me, like narrative change strategy or Black feminist liberation (and I don't have much to offer him when to comes to music creation or particle physics). When I am pissed at him, my friends allow me to vent, but also move me toward empathy and reconciliation. And there is a deep joy and rightness with the world that I get from sitting in the presence of my closest girlfriends, loving one another, laughing, eating, drinking, and being unapologetically ourselves, something that no man will ever give me.

Bella DePaolo writes about and studies being single. "Just think about the way we talk about relationships now," she said to me. "Significant others—*significant* means 'sex partner.' What a weirdly narrow notion of *significant*." When I asked her what her ideal society would be when it comes to relationships, she said it "would be open to people however they want to live their lives, so people who want to put friendships at the center of their lives on the same level as people who want to put family, and people who mostly like their time alone. There would be no legal rewarding or punishing of people depending on whether they were married or not, the way we do now," she said, referring to the thousand-plus federal laws that benefit people who are legally married. "I think it would be wonderful to have a society in which however you wanted to value people in your life, whoever you wanted to prioritize, that you could do that without getting rewarded or punished for doing so."

FOUR

I Love You Till Ashes or Dirt

Family Beyond Blood and Law

The family we make is as important as the family
that makes us.

—MALKIA DEVICH CYRIL

I WAS GETTING READY for a trip to New York, where I'd
stay with my friend Whitney, her husband, and their two
sons. I was showing my son, Solomon, pictures of the two
boys as a small effort to share the experience I'd be having
while I was away from him. "What gender pronoun do they
use?" he asked me. I grinned to myself as I answered, "They
use *he* and *him*." I wish I could take credit for my son's question, but that was all Desiree.

Desiree created and founded a social justice and education
organization that, among many other things, holds a summer
camp that my son attends. It's dreamy. He learns about and
practices social justice while also running around and playing
outside. He comes home filthy and exhausted, correcting me
when I assume someone's gender and schooling me on the
freedom fighters he learns about.

When Desiree speaks, it sounds like there's a quiet song
right behind her words. She conveys warmth and welcome

along with little tolerance for your nonsense. My son, who is often slow to warm to others, feels deep safety with, and loyalty to, her. Those feelings transfer to the collective of adults she's pulled together to staff her organization where safety, belonging, and acceptance are embedded in the culture they've created. The environment she makes for children mirrors her activism—organizing, direct action, and education—and her creation of family, because these aspects of her life are entwined.

Desiree and her siblings grew up in the suburbs of cities in Ohio, Virginia, and Louisiana with their married parents. The conditions of their childhood meant that the support of other adults was critical to their survival. "The church was definitely a place where there were other adults and community who could tell me that I was okay, and I could go get a meal when we didn't have food in the house. And even though they were problematic, we also had some neighbors who filled that role. We're still in contact, and they still play a pretty big parental role for me."

While her relationship with church soured as she reached adolescence and came out as queer, the example provided by some of those neighborhood and church relationships provided a foundation that was amplified in communities she developed as a queer person.

Desiree embraces the long-standing practice in queer and Black communities of creating chosen family. For years, Desiree and her sibling Danni, who is also queer, talked about parenting together more closely than is typical of siblings. "There's a lot of acknowledgment that she will fill in in places where I know I have weaknesses. Like I'm super dyslexic, so she can help the kid to read, and when I'm getting too hippy dippy she can roll me back in, or if the kid needs some linear thinking in their life she can help to balance those things out, because she just knows me so well."

Desiree and Danni implemented their model of sharing care for children when Desiree began informally parenting Malik and his sister Kiara, who are part of a family she's close to. Desiree refers to what she does with the kids as "community foster care." "The goal is that the kids stay with their parents or stay in their parents' lives. But during times like homelessness, or dealing with addiction, or just because of capitalism and poverty, when they're unable to have their kids in their homes and they're not able to parent, Malik and Kiara will come and live with me, and I parent them." During the times the kids have been with Desiree, Danni would regularly take them for the weekend, or Nikita, another member of their close community, would have them overnight once a week. "It's a huge help, which I think all parents should have. It's free care, Nikita loved it, and I would go and play with friends, or go out, or do grocery shopping, or whatever."

The clear distinction that Desiree makes is that this arrangement is not like babysitting or the fun-auntie situation. "The kids are comfortable, they know we are a team, and they are excited about it." Malik and Kiara are growing up experiencing home in multiple households with many caring adults. It's not unlike kids whose parents have shared custody of them and who move from one parent's home to the other's. Malik and Kiara know that if things with their parents become unstable, they will be at home with someone known to them where they get attention, love, and security.

As the relationship with the kids' parents has evolved, Desiree has taken on some more official roles, like being the

primary contact for doctors and schools and helping to navigate public benefit systems. She has expanded her family in
other ways as well, marrying her partner Adrienne and giving
birth to a baby.

Desiree emphasized to me the importance of having an
articulated vision of what you want family and community
to look and feel like, especially if you are trying to do something outside cultural conventions. Adrienne explained that
the underlying standard they articulate is one "where everyone genuinely cares about one another and is helping one
another. And things are not about how much money we can
get, but how do we have as much as we need? And then to
the extent that we have more than we need, how are we helping the rest of our community with those resources?"

I really admire Desiree, Danni, and Adrienne's integrity
and clarity of purpose around family and community, particularly because the pull of heteronormativity is strong. In their
community there have been people who want a collective,
broad family, but struggle to hold on to that vision once they
become part of a couple.

This is one of the things I wrestle with when it comes to
my family too. Our culture is made for, supports, and priv-
ileges the nuclear family I'm part of. Divesting from that
privilege is important because it's unearned and harms other
people. It's also important because privilege in the context of
oppression diminishes your experience and understanding of
life. In a 2003 interview with writer and cultural critic Hilton
Als, Toni Morrison rejects the idea that labeling her work as
"female" or "Black" narrows it or limits its reach and accessibility because "being a black woman writer is not a shal-
low place but a rich place to write from. It doesn't limit my

imagination; it expands it. It's richer than being a white male writer because I know more and I've experienced more."[1] This sentiment resonates with my experience of being a Black woman. It also applies, to varying degrees, to the experience of being marginalized in general. The most liberatory, evolved, boundary-breaking people I know hold identities that are marginalized in some way. And when that marginalization, that experience of being "othered" is focused on your ability to make family, then of course you create other models.

It's people who are barred from entering "mainstream" society and have to build on the edges, who provide visionary, life-affirming examples of what's possible. I'm not romanticizing the suffering, trauma, and bullshit that oppression causes. Nor am I suggesting that everyone who experiences oppression does, or should be expected to, create beautiful, future-facing alternative societies. But people in positions of privilege certainly aren't doing it. The savior volunteerism, the accumulative consumption of wellness experiences, and those treks to Bali and Bhutan to discover purpose and meaning through other people's spiritual practices generally miss the point. I love time spent in the woods or days lying in the sand as opportunities to breathe, reflect, be present, and decompress. But the places we go to escape the distractions and obligations and stressful busyness of our everyday are not where we build our lives. And it is in the mundane, the hardship, and the realness of life that what we've built is tested and refined.

---

1. Hilton Als, "Ghosts in the House: How Toni Morrison Fostered a Generation of Black Writers," *New Yorker*, October 20, 2003, https://www.newyorker.com/magazine/2003/10/27/ghosts-in-the-house.

Educator, writer, and artist Kim Katrin says this about queer folks choosing family: "I personally have never seen family created in the way that I have experienced it in queer and trans communities because I've seen people accept individuals regardless of the massive transformations they may experience in their lives and love them from the beginning to the end." This is counter to the abandonment by family and friends that queer people sometimes experience when they come out. "So many of the kids in my life have been rejected by their churches, they'd been rejected by their schools, by their families, simply because their sexual orientation is not what [their family wanted] or because they identify with a gender [their family] didn't plan or expect." So, other queer folks step in to parent, love, care for, and accept. "I've seen adults adopt other adults and give them parenting and guidance that they never received as children."

American queer history is full of examples of relationships that reveal the power and possibility of chosen family. In the 1980s when HIV swept through so many queer enclaves, caretaking of the sick and dying was done by chosen family. Kim continues, "When biological families walked away from them, when they said you're too gay, this disease is too scary, it was queer and trans people who were showing up and helping people pass on to the next part of their existence."

For queer elders who came of age before reproductive technology was prevalent, chosen family, usually younger people, often stepped up to provide the kind of care and support many people with biological or legally adopted children rely on from their kids.

Queer Ballroom culture has another beautiful example of chosen family. Ballroom culture emerged in Harlem in the

1960s as a response to the racist exclusionary practices of predominantly white balls. Participants join "houses" run by a "parent" who establishes the house rules, provides a place where they live together, develops their "children" as performers for balls, and provides love, care, and safety.[2]

While queer chosen family is building love and community in the face of rejection, Black people in America have built chosen family in large part because of our experience of being forcibly separated from our people. Historically, both queer and Black people (and, of course, queer Black people) have had to contend with laws that constrained our ability to legally claim loved ones as family.

The slave trade built on the mass abduction of Black people from their homes and communities on the African continent. Enslaved people were under constant threat of having loved ones, including children, sold away from them. After emancipation, thousands and thousands of freed Black people searched for their loved ones. Many wrote letters to the Freedmen's Bureau and advertised in newspapers. They were searching for people they'd claimed as spouses in addition to parents, siblings, and caretakers they'd last seen when they were small children, people who they had sometimes not seen for three or four decades. Often loved ones' names had been changed, not just because of marriage (many people got married postemancipation), but when people were sold, new owners would sometimes change an enslaved person's last name, and even their first name. This ad from the

2. In addition to documentaries like *Paris Is Burning* and shows like *Pose*, there is some powerful storytelling and scholarship on ballroom culture. It remains an undertold part of American history. All of us should take it upon ourselves to learn about it.

Southwestern Christian Advocate's "Lost Friends" column, which ran from 1887 to the beginning of the 1900s, is just one devastating example.

> *Mr. Editor—I wish to inquire for my son, Robert Grippit, who left me in the year 1837. He belonged to a man by the name of Raip Grippit. He was seven years old at that time, and was carried away by Edward Grippit, who took him to Kemper county, Miss. I belonged to Raip Grippit at that time, but was afterwards sold to David Burrell. We were living in Liberty, Texas; my name was Sally Ann Grippit, but is now Sally Ann D. Burrell.*[3]

Despite the persistent and erroneous idea that the best family formation is two married people raising children on their own, for hundreds of years Black people have maintained an approach to family that taps into the support, knowledge, and capacity of "the village." So many Black folks are raised not just by their parents but by grandparents, aunties, and friends—finding home in a rotation of houses depending on the season (summers with grandparents), their age (Uncle James is particularly good with teenagers), or other resources (Aunt Viv lives in a good school district). I know so many Black folks who didn't find out until they were grown that Uncle James or Aunt Viv are not the biological siblings of their parents.

---

3. "Lost Friends: Advertisements from the *Southwestern Christian Advocate*," The Historic New Orleans Collection, 2019, https://www.hnoc .org/database/lost-friends/index.html.

For decades, Black families have been described as "broken." This is in part because of the misogyny that insists that children do best when raised in a home with two, "opposite-sex" married parents, not just with their mother. There is plenty of data to dispute this claim and the biased research behind it.[4] But part of what is both harmful and boring about that narrow lens is that misses what is beautiful, resilient, supportive, and brilliant about the breadth and fluidity of so many Black families.

Our villages of play cousins and sister-friends ease the challenging realities most of us face—trying to make ends meet, the daily logistics of life, the need for emotional support—in addition to the relentless stress of living in a racist culture. Journalist Donovan X. Ramsey told me about his mom's network of women who supported one another in many ways, including pooling the contents of their refrigerators to have potlucks to feed their families. "I grew up in this community with all of these Black women that were friends with my mom, and all their lives were intertwined. Some of them worked together, some were cousins, or sisters, or had gone to high school together. It was supportive in ways that I think they didn't let us know as kids, because that wasn't our business to know who was borrowing money, or who was whatever. When I think back to a lot of the pivotal moments, there was Miss Teresa, and there was Miss Toya—they were definitely part of my family growing up."

---

4. See Shawn Fremstad, Đarah Jane Glynn, and Úngelo Williams, "The Case Against Marriage Fundamentalism: Embracing Family Justice for All," Family Story, April 4, 2019, https://familystoryproject.org /case-against-marriage-fundamentalism/.

Sage Crump, a cultural strategist, has a similar experience of family. Her parents met in Detroit and moved to Newark when her father got a job there. Away from biological family, they built new family. "I didn't grow up with this idea of family being blood. There were always multiple folks who were considered family. I have Auntie Em and I have Miss Shirley and I have Auntie Irene. All these people that I wasn't blood related to who have the title and the expectation of family in my life."

Relationships with friends of her mother, women she considered aunties, were ultimately her own relationships, and not contingent on that status of her mother's relationship with them. "Even when she falls out with them, I never fall out with them. They're always my aunties. I'd be like, 'Mommy, I'm going to see Auntie Clarice.' And she'd be like, 'Hmm, okay.' Like clearly she and Clarice are not in cahoots right now. But that has nothing to do with me. I'm going to see Clarice."

My friend, the writer Amber Butts once told me a story about sitting around with her family looking at old pictures, trying to figure out who was blood and who was chosen and ultimately realizing that it didn't matter.

Donovan explained the power in Black people's way of doing family like this: "When you think about what racism, and anti-Blackness in particular, are in America, what their purpose is—it's to exclude us from the greater society, to kill us off. Human beings have been able to persist as a species because we are social. And when a group of people is removed from the greater society, usually that is as a punishment, or it is as a way to kill off that strain of people. And what Black folks have done is to create this alternate society that rivals the majority society so much that they try to adapt and adopt some parts of Blackness. . . . I know that everything in me comes from the society that I was born into. And that includes my family. And I know that I'm literally only alive because of them, that they were that safety net, they were the thing that kept me from all the machinery of the state."

Black people in America have been separated—stolen across an ocean, sold away from our people, pushed from home by everyone's hope for us, snatched up by police and locked in cages, detached by assimilation to education and labor systems, taken by Child Protective Services, abandoned because of unhealed trauma—a million devastations and hearts rended. When our deepest bonds are attacked, there is horrendous damage, there is suffering that is inflicted upon generations of people. But our love, our bond, the things that make us family, that allow us to make family, are not broken. When we are separated, we remake family. We take in those who come to us. We reconfigure with those left behind.

"SOME SHIT GOES DOWN, YOU BETTER TELL ME."

For Tammy, whose adult family life is not anchored by the conventions of marriage and child rearing, this experience of having grown up with chosen family reformed in adulthood. She grew up in a small town in Tennessee called Humboldt. "There was always a sense, like when you walk down the street, you acknowledge people, because that could be family." Like so many other Black folks, Tammy grew up with uncles, aunts, and cousins to whom she didn't know she was not biologically related.

"My family origin, for the most part, was chosen. It wasn't just blood. As I got older and my politics became sharper, and as I continued to get older in my spirituality, being very intentional about choosing who is in that inner circle became a big thing."

What is so powerful and instructional about how Tammy has reconfigured family for herself is the ways in which she takes what was positive and powerful, dumps the garbage (gendered obligations), and fends off external expectations ("if I do something for you, I get to judge you") and assumptions about what her family is or is supposed to be (the "no matter what, you have to do for family" code). "A mother and father are family, so if you don't see them during the holidays, something's wrong, right? No, that's other people's stuff. I realize that now, and can deal with it. I can be intentional, I can differentiate, and that's my choice."

Tammy and I met through our shared social justice movement work. And she has been part of Black Women's Freedom Circle from day one. She brings deep spirituality, wise words, and wry humor into our group.

"One of the things I made a decision about when I left my old job was to put more time and energy to people who are in my circle," she told me. "I decided to stop thinking about having lunch or dinner or whatever with someone as work. I'm going to invest time, energy, and money, if necessary, in other people, even if nothing comes out of it in that moment. That's worth doing."

A diversity of people benefited from this shift in thinking. Among the people Tammy, who is an "evolving heterosexual," considers family are Terry, a white gay man several years her senior, and his son, who is a godson to her. There's

Kevin, a gay Black man who she considers her "spiritual part-ner." And then there's Yvonne, a straight Latinx woman she considers "a spiritual partner and sister-friend." With each of them, she's had explicit conversations about their love for each other, the special place the relationship holds in their lives, and their commitment to it. "That was a verification to each other that this wasn't some passive thing, and that this is blood, and some shit goes down, you better tell me."

In thinking about the explicit communication and boundary-pushing intimacy she has created with her inner circle, Tammy gives some credit to the BDSM[5] community she was part of. "What I liked about it was the expectation that you be very explicit about relationships. Like, *really* ex-plicit: you sit down and have these explicit conversations, not only about sex and 'in the play,' quote, unquote, but even the off hours, whether or not you are allowed to contact me, and if so, then in what context. It really forced those conversa-tions to happen."

The practice of explicit communication she found there countered the fantastical ideas that we learn about relation-ships. "I think we have to deal with the idea that we learn from movies and from norms that say, 'Oh, relationships are so organic. You don't need to say anything. Things so natu-rally happen.' Well no, things naturally fall apart."

That level of smart, open, thoughtful communication re-quires a willingness to be vulnerable that doesn't come easy to everyone. "You're creating a relationship, which is not transactional. You're creating connection and intimacy. I

---

5. Bondage and Discipline, Dominance and Submission, Sadism and Masochism.

think that's why some people try to keep distance—intimacy. What's made my relationships with nonblood family really good and juicy and useful, and just giving me life, is that they're intimate. At the core of it is that I can be vulnerable, and put all my shit out there, and not be judged for it, and have it held. That's explicitly understood."

As with so many of the folks I talked with, Tammy's configuration of family bumps up against the limitations of our national imagination about what family looks like and, therefore, who is included when it comes to policies and practices. The right to marry is one that some groups of people have had to fight for. But we are still quite limited in our ability to access the protections and benefits we should be able to access because our laws are still quite antiquated when it comes to defining family.

From Social Security inheritance regulations to employer bereavement policies, someone else's narrow definition of family restricts the protections and supports we can receive. Even marriage equality fell into the heteronormative trap of what a family looks like and prioritized romantic-partnership love over other kinds of love.

"I was really upset when the marriage equality movement moved the fight away from not only involving gay people, but single women, people taking care of their parents. I was like, 'Wow, you had a bigger coalition, potentially.'"

Tammy is right. Less than half of adults in America are married.[6] (For comparison, in 1960, 72 percent of adults were

6. "Profile America Facts for Features," United States Census Bureau, August 16, 2017, https://www.census.gov/content/dam/Census/news room/facts-for-features/2017/cb17-ff16.pdf.

married.[7]) About 34.2 million of us are providing unpaid care to an adult aged fifty or older.[8] So many of us are kept from wrapping the resources of money, care, and time around the people we consider family. Further, for an ever-increasing number of us, the financial security that allegedly comes from hard work is elusive. As Tammy approaches fifty, figuring out what it will look like to be financially secure as an older person is a struggle.

"As a single woman, what is your future as an elder? Because a lot of the old paradigms don't exist anymore. There's no 401(k) and pension plans, there's no cashing out that house that you lived in for twenty years. That stuff is nonexistent. Even if you believe in it, it doesn't exist anymore. I just think because I'm single, it's more explicit with me."

Our friend Teresa wonders about this too. Now that her son is grown and away at college and Teresa is getting older, she thinks about what kind of family she'll need as she gets older. She worries about the terrible things that a lot of people who live alone worry about as they age—falling and not being able to call for help, dying and no one finding your body for days. But it's also about establishing community postparenting.

"I'm still trying to figure out who my peeps are. When you've been immersed in this whole crazy parenting thing

7. D'vera Cohn et al., "Barely Half of U.S. Adults Are Married—A Record Low," Pew Research Center, December 14, 2011, https://www.pewsocialtrends.org/2011/12/14/barely-half-of-u-s-adults-are-married-a-record-low/.
8. NAC and AARP Public Policy Institute, "Caregiving in the U.S. 2015," AARP.org, June 2015, https://www.aarp.org/content/dam/aarp/ppi/2015/caregiving-in-the-united-states-2015-report-revised.pdf.

and you come out of it, everyone's kind of already established in their little cliquey cliques. The only child in me is like, 'I can entertain myself.' But then I'm like, 'Who do I call when I want to be sad?' That's the moment. I can be happy alone, it's the sadness part. Who's going to hold this space for me and not expect me to be joyful all the time?"

A lot of my single women friends are having this dilemma. They are in their midthirties to near-fifties, they don't have partners, and they aren't willing to settle for what seems to be a pool of people who don't have their shit together politically, emotionally, and/or financially. But they also want sex, companionship, intimacy, someone to talk to at the end of the day, and someone to care for them if they get sick and as they age. Obviously, having a partner is no guarantee that you get and keep any of these things, but it's the model we're sold.

I talked with my friend Liz about it, and asked if she'd thought about disaggregating those roles—sex, companionship, roommate, etc.—and doing most of them with a committed group of good friends. Liz is straight and sex, as far as I can tell, is the only function that requires a man and, it seems to me, that is the easiest thing to access. She said that it was something she was thinking about and had actually talked to a few of her friends about. She also explained that letting go of the idea of a home with a husband and kids requires some grieving and that she really needed to take time for that in order to consider something else.

STRONG SQUAD

"Bar Method doesn't create community. I've been going there for fourteen years taking classes next to the same women and no one knows anyone's name. The owner doesn't even say hello to me." I was waiting for class to start at Pilates Barre & Jams (PB&J!), the studio my friend and the kicker of my ass Teresa created in her home. She was having an open house and these three women who used to take classes from her (at said community-less studio) showed up. I listened silently grinning because it dawned on me that at PB&J, Teresa absolutely creates community.

In anticipation of setting intentions for 2017, I'd been looking for a personal trainer and Teresa was recommend to me by several folks. I reached out, and we made a date for her to come by my house to chat. The person who showed up at my door was a stunning, tall, bald Black woman with big glasses, and a steampunk meets ratchet meets hippie vibe—like Grace Jones if Grace Jones was someone you'd want to snuggle with. She posted herself on the red stool in my kitchen, asked me questions about my goals (get strong—I don't care about how much I weigh), told me about herself and her approach (she doesn't give a shit about weight either), solved my inability to hydrate adequately (I need to use a straw, basically an adult sippy cup), and made me feel excited and determined.

I worked with her one-on-one for months until she opened PB&J and started teaching group classes. Now, three times a week, I earn my place as a proud member of her Strong Squad—this is the community she's built. Teresa has all these funny analogies that she uses to explain how to move or what to pay attention to in our body. She makes us laugh during the pain of working out. She is adamantly body positive and tolerates no body shaming of any kind. She takes great joy in pushing us and in the complaining and cursing that sometimes bursts from the room. I have, many times, said, "Fuck you!" when she adds some horrific, seemingly impossible move to the flow of class, or "This is bullshit!" when the reps are piling up and my muscles are rebelling. She loves it. She loves what she does and takes a kind of wicked joy in the pain she puts us through to make us stronger.

I'm not someone who likes discomfort that leads toward accomplishment. I do not feel any urge to do hard or dangerous things to test how far I can go or prove anything to myself. I will never run a marathon. I will never voluntarily jump out of a plane. I will never fast for days on end. I will never quit eating or drinking anything delicious unless a medical professional insists that it will kill me—and then I will probably start consuming whatever it is again when I'm in my nineties. It's not that I don't think I am capable of these things—I know I am—but I don't want to. Life provides plenty of hardships and trials. I avoid intentionally adding to them. And the truth is that even though I get up hella early several times a week to exercise, I don't always like it. What I like, what I love, actually, is the people I do it with.

Strong Squad leans queer, of color, and politically left. While it's open to anyone, it's not *for* everyone. Teresa's style is not what everybody is looking for. Her body-positive approach is not a gimmick or theory. It's a deep, science-based philosophy that counters our cultural obsession with weight and our worship of a very narrowly defined body standard (yet another hurdle for us to jump to achieve the elusive American Dream). Teresa is Black, queer, polyamorous, a single parent, a former stripper, unmarried, pushing fifty, and unapologetically deeply feeling, loud, and hilarious. She has given the American Dream the middle finger and carves out her own dream life based on who she is and what she wants. She makes room for a bunch of us because she knows she's not the only one who needs an alternative, and none of us wants to do it alone.

"This baby was crying and crying and crying a few seats up, and everybody was just like, 'Ba!' and I was just like, 'Fuck this,' and I got up and I went over and I said, 'Hi, come here,' and the baby was like ??? And the mom was like ??? I said, 'I can't steal your baby because we're thousands of feet in the air. I'm going to take this baby to go hang out with my kid,' and she was like, 'Okay.' We just hung out for a few hours. And I was like, 'I could either have you be screaming or I can just help you just chill. You need a change of scenery and so does your mom.'"

This is one of the things I love about Teresa. She will enthusiastically insert herself into people's lives when she sees a gap. If you're on a plane with her and your baby is crying nonstop, she will come and hold your baby. It doesn't really matter if she knows you or not; she is willing to step in and help you out so you can take a moment to pull yourself together. This is the kind of openness that draws people to her, that allows us to trust her knowledge, expertise, and intentions.

Teresa has all the confidence, self-knowledge, and clarity I imagined middle age would be about when I was in my twenties, but none of the dowdiness, seriousness, and no-fun-ness. She loves horror movies. She goes to those wine and paint classes and hangs the art she makes in her "Shit Show Art Gallery & Bathroom." She knows who she is, but is not settled; she is still growing and learning. She is looking for ways to be herself but also have family she can count on, especially as she ages.

While growing up, Teresa mostly lived with her grandparents. It was her grandmother who made sure holiday celebrations happened and made the house feel warm. "There was love when she was there." When she was eleven, her grandmother died and her mother became a drug addict. Her grandfather kicked her mom out, so it was just him and Teresa. "There was no, 'How are you doing? How is life going?' He barely spoke to me. He would give me money and he would feed me and that was it."

Teresa met Scott in her twenties. She was working as a stripper[9] at various clubs and he worked at one of them. After about a year and a half together, they had a son. One afternoon, Teresa was nursing her son in a chaise lounge. The sun was shining on them and she thought to herself, "Oh, wow, I have to teach this person to be a hundred percent themselves, to always be true to themselves. Don't let anyone fucking tell you no, or that you can't, and that you're not awesome." She immediately asked herself if *she* was modeling what she wanted her son to learn, because, "I can't teach it if I'm not living it." When Scott came home that evening, she told him they couldn't be together anymore.

It wasn't because she didn't love him, but because she finally accepted that she is a lesbian. After days of tears, Teresa moved out of her home with Scott and in with Tanya, a friend who was a single mom. They lived together for about five years, part of which included another mom, Wendy, and

9. Teresa's burlesque work as Simone DeLaGhetto is legendary.

her two kids. "We had this house full of children that played together and moms that drank too much wine." No one ever had to pay for childcare.

"Tanya was a dancer too—we worked at the same place. We would take care of each other's kids. It would be like, 'I have to work tonight, can you . . .' I'm like, 'Yeah, sure.' Or, 'I have to do this thing on Saturday, can you take the kids?' and that person would get the car."

Other than her grandmother, Teresa felt like she really didn't have good examples of how to parent. She and Scott figured out how to coparent and support their son without courts or legal arrangements, in part because neither of them had money to spend on lawyers or filing, but also because they respected and cared about each other. But it was Tanya who helped Teresa become a better parent. "The first time when Tanya gave me the glass of wine and told me to chill out, her daughter was being all crazy and I just didn't know what to do. So, I was freaking out myself and screaming, and it wasn't cool to be screaming at someone's child.

"It was because of her that I learned to have a sense of humor with parenting, because I was just kind of like, 'I don't know what the hell's going on,' and Tanya was like, 'It's all good, they're just kids and they suck and they have their issues.'"

With Tanya and Wendy, Teresa was able to get the emotional and practical support she needed to work, raise her kid, and begin building her life after splitting up with Scott. "You know that whole 'it takes a village'? I really believe that that should be a thing, because when Tanya and Wendy were around and we were living together helping each other with each other's kids, it was brilliant. I had less stress. I could do more, I could do all of the things knowing that there were people I could call who would take care of my kid."

"DON'T BE AFRAID TO GO TOWARDS THAT LOVE."

"It was a total hood place with all these flat yards and these flat-top houses," Darlene explained to me, speaking of Barry Farm, the public housing complex in Washington, DC, where she spent much of her childhood. "You walk up the front steps—two or three of them. There's two doors, one on the left and one on the right, and they go to two separate houses, but they mirror each other." All these identical duplexes had identical front yards—small squares divided by a sidewalk leading to the front steps.

"My grandmother had a wire around her grass. There was no grass anywhere else. Everywhere else there was dirt, there's rocks, there's all kinds of shit going on, but if you came running through that yard like kids did, you were gonna trip your ass up and fall. All the kids had to learn. Eventually you'd see all these kids running crazy though the yards. They'd get to my grandmother's yard and they'd sidestep it and run down the front sidewalk and get past her yard, and they'd keep running through the yards of everybody else."

Darlene's maternal grandmother, Viola, was a domestic worker who raised five children. Her home in Barry Farm was the center of her family's life. Next door, in the house that mirrored her own, lived her best friend, Connie. Connie and Viola raised their children together, creating a merged sense of home and family for their children and grandchildren.

Women like Viola and Aunt Connie were "bad-ass" women who raised their children and held their families together in what Darlene describes as "one of America's top ten worst fucking places in the world to grow up." They did this largely without men.

"Without them even knowing it, they set me up to feel so comfortable to just be myself. For years, I thought my grandmother had never been married because I never saw a man living with her. They chose it. So, I get to choose that for sure. I do not have to make myself think that I have to be married to a man."

This was powerful for Darlene not just because it meant that, as a woman, she didn't have the expectation that to get through life, she needed a man, but that because as a queer person, marrying a man wasn't going to happen anyway. This translated into an orientation toward family that was in keeping with both Black and queer traditions of chosen family. In her early twenties, she became family with her friends; and as they had children, their kids would become family to her as well.

"I get to be an adult that's not the parent, that actually gets to walk through things with these young people, and it's so powerful. That's a joy—knowing that I'm a separate adult that this young person can talk to."

I asked Darlene what she tells the young people in her life about creating family. She said, "Don't allow the constraints of society to trap you." This is exactly how she came to parenthood.

Darlene's partner at the time, Roselyn, was doing work with young people and met Angel. Angel was seventeen and homeless, couch surfing from friend to friend. She'd dropped out of school and was going to night school to get her GED. Roselyn wanted to provide Angel with some housing stability to help her out.

"I said yes, but I didn't know if it was smart," Darlene told me. "What if I needed to kick out a crazy kid?—horrible thought. Well, she moved in and she was anything but crazy. I loved her from those first unsure moments when none of us knew if our decisions were good ones."

After their first weekend living together, Angel decided that Darlene and Roselyn were her mothers and she lived with them for several years. Angel not only had a home and two loving mothers, but she was invited into a vast network of women "and a few men" who gave her a multitude of examples of what a life could be like and who she could be. And she didn't just receive care, she also gave it. When Darlene got cancer, Angel brought her food and stayed with her to support her physical and emotional health.

"I remembered telling her she didn't need to call us anything, but she was adamant. She didn't care what others thought. She didn't care what she had to explain. We'd become mothers to her. This isn't uncommon in people of color queer communities. For us, this arrangement was about everything from home to health care to relationship advice to caring for other family members."

The other thing Darlene told me about making family is, "Don't be afraid to love openly. Don't be afraid to love. If you love somebody, just go for it. Make that family. You don't need to have the right words or the right lexicon or anything like that. Don't be afraid to go towards that love."

Darlene reinforced for me the idea of letting each of our close relationships be its own thing, cocreated by the people in it with its own parameters, ways of expressing love, and roles we play in each other's lives. Cat is my confidant and my historian. Mariah is my teacher and my mirror. Teddy is my coexplorer in understanding who I am and where I want to evolve. They are all family to me. I used to think that was about having people who mirrored some biological family relationship. Sometimes that works—Cat is my sister. But other times it doesn't—I don't think of Teddy as a brother or a cousin, but he's someone I consider family.

THE DEPTH OF CHOOSING

Rebecca's story of family includes both rejection and sep-aration. Rebecca's mother is white and grew up in a large Mormon family in Salt Lake City. For falling in love with a Black man she was disowned by her family and excommu-nicated from the church. After growing up in a community that centered family and church (in this life and the next), this rejection left her hurt and lonely. "When I was a kid," Rebecca told me, "she framed it as, 'well, good, we're better off without them because they're racist. And who needs that?' I saw my mom as this brave person who had chosen to leave this community because she was rejecting these oppressive frameworks and was better than that. But, of course, it's a little more complex than that, because I think if she could've had the community, she still would've."

Rebecca's father wasn't around after she was a baby. He spent much of her childhood incarcerated, so it was just her and her mother. "He would write me letters and send me little things that he made in the woodshop in the prison, you know, like, gifts. I was always angry that my dad wasn't there, especially growing up in Utah where there's a really oppressive definition of what a family should look like, which is this totally not realistic stay-at-home mom, two parents, and not two-point-five kids, but like five kids, and a backyard with a trampoline."

When Rebecca was a senior in college she decided she wanted to get to know her dad, so she reached out to him. He was living in Phoenix with his sister and they arranged a visit. Rebecca hung out with him, her aunt, and cousins and found the experience anticlimactic. After a childhood of anger, she felt deep compassion for all that he'd been through and all he'd missed out on. "We got along fine. We had conversations. He shared some stuff with me about how he understood his relationship to me. It was all kind of almost like the most . . . not ideal, I don't want to say ideal. That's not right. But it was almost the easiest given all the context that could have otherwise made it difficult."

They developed a relationship, staying in touch by phone. Six months after they reconnected, her dad got meningitis and died. "I was really sad, but I was extremely grateful that I had had the wherewithal to make the effort to go meet him and spend time with him because I had no idea that he was going to die six months later. If he'd died, and I'd never known him, that would've been more hurtful, I think. That would've been something more traumatic for me to live with."

While she kept in touch with some of her father's family, she'd never met his sons—her brothers. (Both of Rebecca's parents had children from previous marriages.) She had a brother in Utah who'd been raised by his maternal grand-mother. He didn't know Rebecca existed and had been told that their dad was a terrible person. After her father's funeral, she decided it was time for them to be in touch. After some searching, which her mother helped with, Rebecca called him to introduce herself. The next time she was home from school, they arranged to meet.

"I met him and his four kids. He's awesome and his wife is awesome and his kids are awesome. And he thinks I'm awesome. I think he was more perplexed than I was because he was like, 'I just always thought that everything related to my father was going to be a bad thing, and basically I have this awesome sister.'"

He is now the sibling Rebecca is closest to. They spend holidays together and Rebecca is an involved aunt with his kids. After meeting as adults they made each other family.

In 2017, Rebecca was researching her family's genealogy and was particularly interested in finding relatives, using a DNA test. Her understanding was that this is easier if you have a paternal male relative's sample. So, Rebecca asked her brother if he'd send in the swab if she set it up. He said yes.

The service she used automatically matches you with any blood relatives in their system, but in looking at her results and then her brother's, she didn't find a match. Rebecca looked repeatedly at the results, lining up the paternal side—no match. She called the company, and after an awkward conversation—because this happens frequently—they confirmed that she and her brother are not biologically related.

"I was devastated, sobbing, because to me this man is my brother. And he has been my connection to my father. And even though my brother doesn't identify with my father and never knew my father, who my brother was as a person gave me hope about who my father could've been. I always saw my brother and my brother's family as hopeful—this is what would have been possible if circumstances were different."

Rebecca was scared she was going to lose her brother, and it also called into question her connection to her father. "I called my mom and I'm like, 'Mom. Are you sure that my dad is my dad?' And my mom chuckled and she was like, 'Yes. I'm sure. He was living in my house. When I got pregnant, he was the only person I was having sex with, so I'm pretty sure.'"

Rebecca decided to deliver the news to her brother in person, so she waited a few months until she was home again from grad school. They met at his house while his kids and wife were out. "I said to him, 'So, if I found something out from the DNA test that radically changes our understanding of things, would you want to know?' Because one of my friends had been like, 'Maybe you should ask him first if he wants to know.'" Her brother said yes as he watched Rebecca tear up. Rebecca pulled the results up on her computer to show him and didn't say anything. "To me, this is a dramatic reveal. I was so wound up about it."

Rebecca's brother was a little surprised, but unfazed. "He gave me a hug and he was like, 'Dude, you're still my sister. I love you. You're a part of our lives. You've been a part of our lives since my kids were little. You've been their aunt their whole lives now.'"

One of the things I take away from Rebecca's story is the depth of choosing. They chose each other as favorite siblings when they thought they were biologically related. They remain each other's favorites despite the absence of biological

connection. So many of us struggle with feelings of obliga-
tion toward people just because we are related to them. This
sometimes compels us to stay in relationship with people. But
we do not have to stay attached to our given (as opposed to
chosen) families. What Rebecca, and so many others, model,
is that we do get to choose. And those commitments can be
as deep as we expect legal or biological commitments to be.
It's really up to us.

Sage Crump put it this way: "One of the things a good
friend and I always say is, 'I love you till ashes or dirt.' Often-
times those types of commitments are only framed in romantic scenarios. But we're really explicit. We're going to work
this thing out, we're going to work it out because we're not
abandoning each other ever. And that means there have been
times where, yup, you know we are till ashes and dirt and I
will call when I'm ready to talk again." This kind of commitment underscores the deliberateness she finds necessary
for creating and maintaining chosen family. "At this stage of
my life, it doesn't happen haphazardly, it doesn't happen by
accident. It's an intention to make space and room, both to
be in the same place to physically engage with folks, but also
to be clear that in this invitation to be family, I hold myself
accountable to show up for them."

FIVE

The Best of the People We Know

The Village We All Need

The village is not just a space for children to be
nurtured; it is the core of our human existence.[1]
—MALESHA JESSIE TAYLOR

I REMEMBER A CONVERSATION I had with my friend
Johnny about why he and his wife had so little time for
themselves, individually or together. He shared with me the
litany of activity that took up the majority of their waking
weekday hours—working, getting to and from work, getting
their kids to and from childcare, and caring for their kids.
Once the kids were asleep at night, they had to take care of
things like laundry, cleaning, bill paying, etc., before falling
into bed too exhausted to talk much past logistics for the next
day, much less have the kinds of conversations that maintain
emotional intimacy or have sex. Weekends were a little better, but there was still grocery shopping, fixing things, and
household chores, and their ever-present children, both under the age of five.

---

1. Malesha Jessie Taylor, "What a Move to the 'Burbs Taught Me About
Community," Mater Mea, June 27, 2016, https://www.matermea.com
/blog/building-a-village-after-moving-to-the-suburbs.

As I listened to him, bits of advice kept surfacing, partly formed in my mind. But it all sounded like the many, many articles I'd read about processes or products that are meant to save time, organize our lives, and provide some reprieve from the relentless everything that is the life of two working people raising children. And I knew from my own experience that most of those articles were trash because they focused on routines, processes, or gadgets that didn't address the underlying problem two working people trying to raise kids on their own have: not enough people.

For Nino and me, the years before both of our kids hit five included the birth of our second child, two moves, buying a house, me changing jobs twice, Nino starting a business, death and illness in our families, and a whole lot of other uproar. When we were at our best, our saving grace was other people. And when, because of circumstance or our own shortsightedness (usually not asking for help), we didn't have that support, it showed. Neither of us grew up in the context of an insular nuclear family, so when our attempts to do the insular nuclear family thing butted up against the realities of modern American life, we had a model to reach for: the village.

Johnny and his wife had no village. Johnny's mom was nearby and helped occasionally, but she was not interested in being a regular source of childcare. They did not have close relationships with other adults who could pitch in; even if they had, it wouldn't have occurred to them to ask for help. Like so many "successful" couples, they believed that being able to raise small children is part of what a couple can handle on their own. I remember Johnny saying, not without a little panic in his voice, "We are so lucky by most accounts. We have really good jobs. We're healthy, our kids are healthy. We can afford our home and childcare and a car. Why is this so hard?" I said, "Dude. You're not supposed to do it alone." And I told him about one of the best things I ever did for my family: Kid Fun.

It is really date night for parents, but I called it Kid Fun to sell it to the kids. When Solomon was two and Stella seven, Nino and I could count on one hand the number of dates we'd had since Solomon's birth. Not having adult time was putting a strain on our relationship. And I thought, *We are not the only ones with this problem.* We knew lots of other parents who had multiple little kids and few options for getting away from them. We occasionally paid for childcare, but if I wanted a really nice date—which I do, because I'm bougie— then paying for babysitting *and* dinner/drinks/a movie wasn't something we could do often. I also wanted to remove as much of the planning from the process as I could. I wanted a consistent date night that would show up on our calendars and that we could count on.

I reached out to two other families I liked—our kids went to school together—and proposed a simple process. Every other Saturday, one family would get all seven kids. The other parents would have four blessed hours to do whatever. We'd rotate. Having regular date nights (which were sometimes stay-in-and-order-takeout-and-have-sex-while-it's-still-light-out nights) was fantastic. Just that little bit of regular time alone together, not talking about logistics, not in the too-tired time between the kids' bedtime and ours, allowed for regular, real adult connection.

Those years when the kids are new can be really rough on a couple's relationship. Reworking the balance of focus, roles, duties, and everyone's relationship to one another is something most of us aren't prepared for. I had been told about it—and then experienced it—and I still wasn't prepared for it the second time. I did know enough to want to make space for Nino and me to find our way back to each other after the initial upheaval of kid number two. Even on the Saturdays when it was our turn to watch the kids, we experienced the surprise bonus of alone time because the kids were entertaining each other. We'd hide out in the kitchen eating pizza, drinking a glass of wine, and making each other laugh and telling stories.

And it became clear to me early on that my kids benefited as well. I remember picking up my kids from Chris and Ellen's home—Solomon must have still been under three. I walked in the house and saw Chris holding him. They were laughing, and looking at each other with a fondness that made me catch my breath. In that moment, I saw how valuable it was for my children to have these relationships with other adults.

Although my earliest memory is before my parents got divorced (my first ice cream), I have a vivid memory that made me realize how potentially tenuous my life had been made by their splitting up. I think we were looking for a new apartment. I remember my mom sitting on the steps outside an apartment, crying. I'm not exactly sure what had happened, but I do remember feeling in my three- or four-year-old self that we were terribly, deeply alone.

Because my mother was orphaned as a child and the rest of her family disowned her when she married my dad, when my parents split up my mother had no family and very little community to support her. I don't doubt that the fear and loneliness I felt standing on those steps watching my mother cry was reflective of what my mother felt, despite also feeling liberated from an unworkable marriage. But she did what single moms do and she built a life for us, in part, by building us a family.

Women raising children without the support of a second parent—a.k.a. single mothers—are among the most demonized, shamed, and penalized family structure in America because of the misogynist idea that a woman with a child but without a man is a slut (which we're supposed to understand as a bad thing)—and those negatives are multiplied if she is poor and Black. If heterosexual, white, middle-class families with kids are America's gold standard, then poor, unmarried, Black mothers are vilified as its disgrace.

We say "raised by a single mom" to suggest all kinds of unarticulated things. It's meant to suggest deprivation, hardship, and poverty born of moral deviance or bad choices. Occasionally it's meant to inspire sympathy or inspiration for a child who is "beating the odds." Whatever it conjures up, so clear are the negative connotations that some women who decide to have and raise kids without a partner find it necessary to set their families apart by designating themselves "single mothers by choice." A simplistic and problematic distinction, to be sure. But women becoming mothers without being married is increasingly prevalent. According to the Pew Research Center, "The share of U.S. children living with an unmarried parent has more than doubled since 1968, jumping from 13% to 32% in 2017."[2] While there's been a small

2. Gretchen Livingston, "About One-Third of U.S. Children Are Living with an Unmarried Parent," FactTank, Pew Research Center, April 27, 2018, https://www.pewresearch.org/fact-tank/2018/04/27/about-one-third-of-u-s-children-are-living-with-an-unmarried-parent/.

increase in the number of men solo parenting, most of those parents are women. And because more women who are white and well off financially are doing it and being public about it, it's become more socially acceptable for them (that acceptability hasn't extended to Black and/or poor moms). But women have been successfully raising children without men in their homes for ages. Solo parents' practices and thinking about how to do this have a lot to teach us—not just those of us solo parenting, but anyone raising children.

My father was in my life, but my mother raised me with the help of others. Single parents often figure out what coupled parents never do: it takes many caring adults to raise kids. From the logistics of transportation and meals to emotional support to modeling a diversity of ways to live a life, kids do well when they've got people beyond their parents or primary caretakers in their lives.

AUNTIES

"I knew I wanted to be a mom from a pretty young age. Even as early as college I was thinking about fostering. So when I got married, both of us were on that path initially of having kids as soon as possible." While Naomi's wife wanted to have a child that was biologically related to them, Naomi was much more interested in adoption. When they got divorced, even though she was heartbroken, Naomi also felt that it liberated her to become a mom in the way she wanted to.

She immediately started calling foster care agencies and calendaring orientations and preparing for the home study becoming a foster parent requires. Once she had fulfilled all of the requirements, there was a lot of waiting.

She got a call about three siblings on a Wednesday; Saturday, they'd be coming to stay for the weekend. "I had to really quickly get my house ready to be approved for these kids coming. I didn't have much time to think about it. Then when I picked them up, they were so friendly and instantly sweet and chatty and I think we went into this whirlwind of excitement with each other. It felt like instantly we got along really well." When she dropped them off at their temporary foster mom's home, her apartment suddenly seemed too quiet.

For the next month and a half, Naomi would drive out to see them—spending the day with them, taking them on adventures, getting to know them. When they finally moved in with her, the delight she took in them came through whenever she talked with me about them. But Naomi admits to underestimating how hard the move would be for the girls and how difficult those first several months would be as she went from fun parent to regular parent. The upside to being a single parent is that all the decisions are hers. She parents according to her own timeline, her own discipline style, her own opinions about nutrition, school, activities, medical care, and the myriad other decisions people who parent together often have to come to agreement about. "If you like to be in control, it's kind of nice not having anybody else to have to talk with about it."

I heard this sentiment from a lot of single parents. The time and energy it takes to engage in the process of decision-making can be a lot. Some of the downside came as a bit of a surprise to Naomi.

"The cons are about how you maintain an adult life while having children—on a budget. It's a simple thing like going out to get drinks with a coworker, or the other day I was invited at three o'clock to see a Warriors game with a client, and I'm like, yeah, no. Because that requires getting a babysitter, and it requires paying for that babysitter, and while there are some friends who are willing to watch them, the last-minute nature of it means it's unlikely that they would. Or if they can, it means I have to take them to a friend's house rather than the friend coming to my house, and if it's nighttime, then they need to go to sleep. So, it's all the logistical pieces, but also the financial piece of paying someone else."

This aspect of parenting continues to be among the most challenging for all caregivers, whether they are single parents or two people. We need care for kids—both during hours while we are at work or school—and at times when we need to run errands, go to appointments, care for elders, get exercise, go out on dates, or the endless other things adults need and want to do without kids. People providing that care professionally should be paid well—they often have their own families to support and their own childcare expenses. And collectively, we could do a better job of consistently showing up for parents so they can maintain their relationships and their physical and emotional health while they are raising small people.

Naomi and the girls have a person in their lives who provides both paid and unpaid care. Myra and Naomi are part of the same friend group. When Myra's unemployment was about to run out and she was figuring out her next move, Naomi asked if she would be interested in being a nanny for her kids. Myra has become a member of the family, but not in the way wealthy people say their nanny is a member of the family. Naomi pays Myra for the time she spends with the girls when Naomi needs childcare. But Myra also spends time with them when she wants to, or when she and Naomi are spending time together as friends, with and without their group of friends.

Myra's presence has also made Naomi a better parent. "She's such a compassionate person that it's been this really nice balance for me. Sometimes I feel like I have to do all this boundary setting with them while at the same time trying to remember to infuse that boundary setting with a little more of the hugs and kisses and love. Of course, it's love with the boundary setting but in a different experience for them." Myra is all about infusing the boundary setting with expressions of love.

As a new single parent, Naomi realized she needs others to help care for her kids so she can have a life—and that it might be even more important that those people are reliable and consistent because the girls' first few years were largely unstable. "I don't really have the group that I was hoping a few people might make, which is a more consistent showing up to take care of the kids." There are definitely aunties, people who come over and help with dinner, braid hair, play on the floor, and take them on outings. But as one of the only parents in her peer group, there's a learning curve for the aunties.

In an article I published a few years ago, "In Praise of the Auntie," I wrote, "Aunties are the rule-breakers. When they come over to babysit, the fancy dishes come out, the kitchen becomes a playground, and screen time and bedtime extend. They go on adventures, take my kids to slightly inappropriate

movies and shows, and they expose them to new music."[3]
But, in my experience, aunties (and other nonparenting caretakers) also see children as whole people in a way that parents
don't. It means they can engage with kids as they really are
and see what they are capable of. The mirror they hold up
allows kids to think more deeply about who they are and extend themselves into the world more.

When we spoke, even though Naomi didn't yet have the
community arrangement she wanted, she had a vision of it.
"In my ideal world, I would have a few other people who are
totally okay with just showing up. I have a few friends like
that. They might text me when they're outside the house, but
they're basically literally showing up at my doorstep. . . . Or
they're like, I'm five minutes from your house, what are you
doing? I really love the friends who are kind of less boundaried in that area. I do think that being able to surround
yourself with people who are willing to insert themselves into
your life—the people who just show up—is important."

When she told me this, I immediately thought about
the people who would hate this (*raises hand*). But then I
thought about how hard it is for us to ask for help, certainly
over and over, or to even know what help we need. Some of
us do not want anyone inserting themselves into our lives.
But I wonder how much of that is because we don't have
people who are close enough to us to do it in the right way.
My mother-in-love, Jacque, can be meddlesome and she can
drive me bananas with her well-meaning invasiveness, but

3. Mia Birdsong, "In Praise of Aunties," Slate, May, 6, 2016, https://
slate.com/human-interest/2016/05/in-praise-of-the-auntie.html.

she really gets it right a lot. What Naomi, like so many of us, is asking for, is for people to be close enough to us that they can anticipate our needs, know what we want, and take their place in our lives. But it also means that many of us have to let go of some of our orientation toward privacy and seclusion.

I heard from several folks that this is what they want or this is what they do with their loved ones. There is a balance to strike between offering support versus just providing support in the absence of requests for it. Sometimes people will say no, sometimes they will not appreciate how you inserted yourself. But if we learn our loved ones, if we communicate our feelings and preferences, I imagine we'll do a better job.

THEY KNOCK ON MY DOOR FOR HELP

My friendship with Caroline is one of my longest since moving to California. I was so excited when she asked me to be a godmother to her daughters. We didn't talk about what that meant—were there obligations or tasks?—but it felt like an honor that might be akin to being that fun, but steadily present, aunt. To be real, I've thought about having Damasia and Aleja spend time with me way more often than I've actually made it happen (they do live an hour-plus away from me). But being a godmother has instilled in me a kind of commitment that persists despite my failure to have sleepovers and take them on adventures. I may not be a frequent presence, but I am definitely known.

Caroline, who is white and queer, is raising mixed-race Black Latinx girls. She knows that there are experiences, perspectives, and modeling that people like me can provide for them that she can't. It means recognizing that other people are critical for her daughters' healthy identity development (which is true for all kids, but particularly true for transracial caregivers and kids), and then making sure that happens.

She took them to a Martin Luther King Day celebration and march for kids organized by Abundant Beginnings, a Bay Area social justice group. At the event, the leadership of Black children was centered and supported, which meant, among other things, they lead the parade that was part of the day. For Caroline, that meant allowing her kids to step forward, while she stepped back. "I just had this very kind of spiritual moment where they were in the front of the march holding the sign. I had this really moving moment of just watching them go forward and be surrounded by all of these incredible people that they'd been interacting with during the teach-in and being like, 'Yeah, there are going to be things that you're going to get from Black people. There's this experience that I want you to have—that feeling of whatever your identity is, however you hold all of those pieces—that you have opportunities to be in situations where each of those pieces finds a home. And that I don't need to do that in every way. I just need to make sure that you have access to those experiences within our community.'"

Caroline was with the girls' father, Lázaro, for eleven years, parting when their girls were seven. It was not an easy breakup, and Lázaro, who struggles with mental health issues and self-medicates to manage those issues, has not been able to be a very present parent. When they split up, Caroline was halfway through graduate school and wondered if she was going to be able to finish. "But my mom and her husband totally came through and helped me, making sure my kids weren't just taken care of logistically, but in this time that was very emotionally vulnerable for all of us, that they had these people that were a really great support for them."

The culture of the family that Caroline grew up in was private; you didn't talk about your business outside of the family. She had to push against that to get the support she needed and build the community she wanted for herself and her daughters. She was already feeling the heartbreak and shame of ending a relationship and letting go of the picture of family that she'd spent so long working on. Admitting that she needed help on top of that created additional vulnerability and discomfort. "There were a lot of things within that relationship I had been doing by myself and not talking about. And I think that it was profound to come to a point where I was like, 'Nope, no more secrets about this.' I'm just going to be out here in my messiness and be like, 'I need help.'"

She began opening up to classmates and friends and asking for both emotional support and practical help. "I remember this one time that a friend left food on my porch spontaneously. And it was overwhelming to me because I hadn't had a baby, there hadn't been a death in my family, but there was this huge transition, and she really recognized that."

This shift in openness has her focused on spending more time with friends and "having that be a value that is not just 'kind of like a value' in theory." In turn, Caroline is working on how to notice when her friends could use some support so she can provide something specific. She offers a helpful way to think about approaching that. "There's labor involved in people articulating their needs sometimes that is exhausting when you're already down. And I think without taking people's autonomy or initiative away from them, I am trying to be more specific in terms of how I offer support to people. 'I want to come and do your dishes and throw some laundry in. Would that be okay with you?' Or 'I know this is really hard. Can I maybe look into where you could get some resources for this?' Or 'Can I take your kids? Because I'd really love to have them today while you go do something for yourself.' Or whatever it is."

Being more open about the parts of her life that were hard diminished the fear she had around those things because she felt less alone in her experience. "It's been significant for me to be like, 'Hey, let's turn things over in the light of day.' It doesn't look quite so scary, and I realize that I'm not on my own. Just being able to share in some of those common challenges and joys is really powerful for people. And I think that's true around anything. Having community, having relationship, having connection, having normalization of your experience, sharing in that is really powerful."

Caroline, who is a therapist working in community mental health, applies her practical experience as a therapist to her own situation. "So much of resilience comes out of some kind of trauma—societal trauma or an individual trauma. It's so important to not say, 'Oh, it's a good thing that you had all that trauma in your life because it made you a really resilient person,' and we wouldn't ever intend to create a traumatic experience for our kids. But that they're having some obstacles and things that they have to work through actually builds them into people who are both resilient and empathetic."

When she reflects back on the hardship of the years since she and Lázaro broke up and he became absent from the girls' lives, she recognizes that in spite of how painful it's been, it's also been an opportunity for them to reflect on their own growth—particularly in the context of the other supportive relationships that they've had. "Not only do we have the capacity to do hard things, right, and get through hard things—and not this kind of 'buck up and get through it sort of thing'—but it's how do you get through those things in a way that is relational and connective."

The empathy that hardship can develop is evident when Caroline reflects on the wildfires that her community experiences during California's now-regular wildfire season. Becoming a single parent has made her pay more attention to the challenges other people might have. "It made me realize, who don't I know on my street? Who have I not introduced myself to? Who maybe has some needs that would make it hard for them to be notified about evacuations? All these things that I hadn't thought of—people that sleep without hearing aids in, or that don't have a car so they can't get out quickly if they needed to. It made me go around to meet people that I hadn't met before. There is a way that those kinds of experiences can bring out the best in people."

She told me about a conversation she had with Lázaro's sister when they went to visit his family. "They grow tobacco in their town. And I asked her, 'What happens when there's a bad crop?' I was curious if it impacted the government or if it impacted the farmer. And she didn't even answer that part of the question. She was like, 'It impacts everybody because I know if my neighbor is not doing as well, they have to come knock on my door for help.'"

"WE'RE UPSTAIRS, DOWNSTAIRS, YOU FEEL ME?"

Takema is a fast talker. I imagine it's necessary because her mind moves at a quick pace and she's just trying to keep up. We used to cochair a board of directors together. We would meet up with an agenda and hours later find we'd not gotten past the first item because we'd ended up talking about our kids or dating or marriage or work or politics. There was usually wine and we usually had to schedule another meeting to actually get through our agenda. I love talking with her. She is about the business as a mom. Takema works in education and her kids' academics are paramount and there is no slacking when it comes to school. She supports their talents and loves them deeply and decisively. She raises her three kids with an approach that mirrors how she was raised—single mom with a support system of extended family.

Takema grew up in San Francisco. Her mom worked two jobs and Takema spent a lot of time with her grandparents, who lived close by. Sundays were for family and food. Multiple grandparents and stepgrandparents, her "cool uncles," and others gathered to share a meal. That family members who'd been together and split up came over with current spouses and partners and everyone was considered family was normal to Takema. Although the nuclear family was what she wanted for herself, she also remembers knowing that if she was a single mother, she'd be fine just like her mother was.

Takema met Mario when they were both in Atlanta for a teacher-training summer program. They stayed in touch, met up a few times, and started a long-distance relationship before Takema moved to New York, where Mario lived. They broke up several months later, on September 10, 2001.

Takema was on the bus the next morning when she heard about planes hitting the Twin Towers. As chaos erupted, she ended up at Mario's family's house in the Bronx. "We were like, 'Oh my god, the worst terror attack that's ever happened, happened. We broke up over something trivial, right? And we can't break up; we have to be together.' That was September, and Yasmin was born in December of 2002. That's how our family was made."

They soon moved to the Bay Area, where Takema's family was. They stayed together until Yasmin was eighteen months old. "I think my mom being a single mother let me know that I can do this on my own. I was dead set on just being good and being happy more than being in a relationship, but my mom's strength let me know that I could leave."

While in retrospect Takema thinks they should have worked at the relationship more, she also felt like it freed her up. "I was like, 'Okay, now that we're split up, I'm going to explore all my dreams.' Because you know when you are in a partnership, you're trying to mold your shit with their shit. There was stuff I wanted to do, and I was always trying to check in with him and see if he was okay. Things just opened up for me once I got out. Some birds can't be caged."

A few years later, Mario and Takema reconnected and had a son. A few years after that, she ran into Joseph, someone she'd dated over a decade earlier. "I bump into him at a festival, and then bump into him again a month later. Then I ended up having Little Joe. We were never in a relationship, or planning to get married, or doing any of those things, but I had Little Joe."

This group of adults made it all work. Takema's children's fathers and the fathers' families and her own family are all part of her children's lives. "Every Christmas from the time that I was pregnant with Little Joe, Mario's family always bought gifts for him. When Mario's mom came from New York to visit, she brought gifts for Little Joe. That's family right there."

While Takema is the primary legal parent for Little Joe, she has a shared coparenting relationship with Mario, whose longtime partner also helps raise the kids. Little Joe has regular visits with his dad and Joseph's mom took care of Little Joe for a couple of years when Takema went back to work after Little Joe was born. Takema's own mother lived in San Francisco and played less of a caretaker role in her grandkids' lives until she was displaced from San Francisco and found herself living close to Takema's house in an in-law apartment owned by one of Takema's closest friends. "I go over there, we're upstairs, downstairs, you feel me?"

When I asked Takema about her life now compared to what she imagined being married would be like, she had this to say: "Although companionship and partnership is still important to me, I think what is better is that I'm living in my full self, right? I get to be fully me, good or bad. I get to really just be free to do my own self-discovery, and to live the way I want to live, which is just true to my nature. I get to be true to me, and my kids get to see that. I just took the kids to LA for their birthdays, and we stayed by the pier in Santa Monica. If I had a husband, we'd have to talk about it. We'd have to negotiate it. It's like, I've got money, I work hard, and I get to live with my children. Whatever vision I had in my late twenties about mother, father, children, all living in the house, I think is not the life that was meant for me. I believe that things have totally worked out better for me than this nuclear family that I envisioned."

While the hardship and challenge of single parenting is real, we tend to conflate that hardship with an assumption of aloneness. But what I have heard from so many of the single parents I talked with is that when they have help raising their kids from coparents, friends, and family, they get some of the alone time many of us crave, plus time with others when they want it. Regardless of whether one parents inside or outside of a couple, kids and their parents do better when multiple adults are involved in raising the kids.

And those multiple adults do better too. I remember having the realization that Mariah gets something out of spending time with Stella. And then I felt like a jerk because of course she does—Stella is awesome and Mariah loves her. For parents, the support we need from others to help us raise our kids can feel like a chore to be done, but that's because we need a break or some help. It's easy to forget that those helping adults get to spend time with these kids we love. They get to build relationships with them and those relationships, like Sage's relationships with her mother's friends, like Stella's relationship with Mariah, can become their own. I think about this a lot more now that Stella is a teenager and texts with her aunties about school or plants or Halloween costumes. And I feel that sweet heartache that colors so much of parenting—it's a mix of pride and joy that your kid is growing and evolving, with sadness because that growth is largely away from you. And I'm so grateful that it is toward people I love and trust.

"I'M ROCKIN' WITH YOU TO THE END."

"Before having a child, I said really clearly that I wanted to raise a Black girl that felt free," Kim Katrin explained to me. "So often through our lives, we're heavily policed about what we wear or how we sit or how we talk, and I wanted her to have as much of her life as possible really surrounded by people who will encourage her—'Take up more space, sit how you want to, run where you want to, play with whoever you want to'—really allowing her to explore the fullest potential of the person that she could be."

Kim is a writer, educator, and artist. She's married to Tiq Milan, a writer and advocate. Tiq told me once that the most important thing his mother taught him as a child was, "There was no place in the world that I didn't belong. No matter what people told me, no matter what I saw on TV, everything in this world belonged to me."

This was not an adaptation of a colonial approach that claims possession over other people's things, but a declaration that he was no less than any other child, and anything he saw that he wanted to do or be about was for him, not just for white people or wealthy people. Because his own identity as a Black transgender man is deeply self-determined, he wants his parenting to offer that same capacity to his child. "I want to raise my kid with queer thinking—that you can be whoever you want. Your body is yours. Your identity is yours."

Kim explained to me that her queerness inherently made "respectable Blackness"[4] inaccessible to her, so she never got

---

4. For more on "respectability politics," try Damon Young, "The Definition, Danger and Disease of Respectability Politics, Explained," The

caught in the trap of trying to meet those standards. "Queer black women in particular have created the most beautiful alternative versions of communities and families because of the way they're like, 'I'm not respectable, I'm not trying to be respectable, I'm trying to be here, I'm trying to be whole, I'm trying to be loved, I'm trying to be who I am.' I've always embraced that. I'm never going to fit into those kinds of standards, so why would I try? Why wouldn't I just keep seeking more and more people who love me as I am as opposed to trying to be in a community that would never accept me?"

I met Kim and Tiq in 2016 when they codelivered a beautiful talk called "A Queer Vision of Love and Marriage."[5] But I was already a fan when I met them.

I'd been following Kim on social media and got to witness what she shared as their relationship and marriage unfolded. It was fitting, since they met and fell in love via social media. The visibility of a Black queer couple—a trans man and a cis lesbian—falling in love, getting married, and becoming parents is a rare public story. It would be easy to dismiss a relationship born and shared on social media, but that would be missing the point entirely. As Kim said, "We open up little windows into our relationship for our community to bear witness, and we do this because we want to make maps to the future and not monuments to ourselves."

Root, March 21, 2016, https://www.theroot.com/the-definition-danger-and-disease-of-respectability-po-1790854699, or this Wikipedia entry: https://en.wikipedia.org/wiki/Respectability_politics.

5. Tiq Milan and Kim Katrin, "A Queer Vision of Love and Marriage," October 2016, TEDWomen video, https://www.ted.com/talks/tiq_milan_and_kim_katrin_milan_a_queer_vision_of_love_and_marriage.

When they decided to become parents, Kim and Tiq thought a lot about the community of people they wanted their child to be raised by. "It was very, very important to us that there were lots of Black women of all types around to set an example and to love her and to help us raise her," Tiq told me. "We really looked at the best of the people that we knew in our lives and wanted to make sure that they had a connection to her. People who are really grounded. People we knew so if, God forbid, something happened to me and Kim, they could take care of our child and she'd be okay and she'd be raised in a way that would mirror how we would raise her."

In addition to their biological family, they included people from the extensive Black, queer community they have— women and gender-nonconforming people, elders, caregivers, godparents, and a whole interwoven fabric of folks who are in their lives to support them and their daughter Soleil, and to be examples of what is possible for her.

Kim and Tiq are consistent adults in the lives of other people's children as well. Tiq has three older sisters who have several children. In his family, the men are around, but, as in many families, it's primarily the women who nurture, organize, and make sure things run. "There's so many emotional things going on, whether it's people dying or people having babies or people going to jail or people arguing or events to be planned or things to keep the family progressing and keep the family together, activities that we do to bond—it's always the women who are making those decisions." His parents divorced when he was very young, and while his father was always a part of his life, it was his mother who was the primary caretaker. So, Tiq is also showing his twelve nieces and nephews that men can be nurturing, be part of the things that make a family progress and hold them together.

Kim and Tiq are clear about what they've signed up for as partners and parents. They work really hard on their own relationship, but if for some reason they decided to split up, they have committed to being family regardless. "If it comes to a point where we can't live under the same roof, I'm always going to be where my kid is. If you're the mother of my child and you're in Toronto, well, I'm in Toronto. You're in LA; well, I'm in LA because this is my family," Tiq told me. And Kim echoed this: "Even if we do decide that we're not going to have a romantic relationship somehow in the future or we want to get divorced, we're still family forever, we're parenting forever and there isn't anyone I'd rather do that with."

This kind of commitment to their family, no matter what form it's taking, is refreshing. They aren't blinded by their love for each other or afraid to jinx their relationship by talking about the possibility of their marriage not working out. Instead, they embraced the uncertainty of the future and agreed on what is most important to them.

Kim told me, "Becoming a parent for me is the best thing I have ever done in my entire life, I love every single little bit of it. It has given me a sense of permanence and grounding that I never knew before. I could never imagine something being around forever. I felt like everything was transient. But Soleil is forever, so the family I build around Soleil is forever. This is really exciting for me. I feel like I've rooted for the very first time in my life."

Part of Kim's sharp clarity around this commitment is knowing so many queer people who were rejected by their families, their parents in particular. This is unfathomable to her. "As someone who has worked as a frontline worker in the LGBT community, there have been countless times in the middle of the night where I'd get a call from someone letting me know that their parents found them, found a picture or an image or found their Facebook account, found out they're gay and said that they are disowned. Literally from that moment, they decide you are no longer family. After having a daughter, I can't imagine anything that Soleil could do or say that would make me abandon her in any capacity. Even if she did something that was wrong I would still be like, that wasn't good but I'm here. I'm rockin' with you to the end because you're my child."

In many of the conversations I had, people shared their belief about permanence and longevity when it comes to relationships. It varied—these things are different for everyone. But I get Kim's commitment to her child. My kids are the only people I am committed to unconditionally.

NOBODY WANTS TO HEAR STORIES OF A HAPPY SINGLE MOM

C. Nicole Mason works in the academic and policy fields and is mother to twins. In many ways, it was a bold choice for her to decide to become a single mother. She was born to a teenage mother, grew up poor, and, like me, I think, had to push back against all the assumptions people made about who she was and what she was capable of because they believed all of the stereotypes attached to Black, poor, and teen moms. Even though she has a PhD and is financially well off, she's still a Black woman and no amount of achievement or respectability prevents people from slinging their racism and sexism. Nicole wrote a memoir, *Born Bright: A Young Girl's Journey from Nothing to Something in America*, about growing up poor and navigating her way toward success.[6] It also investigates the systems and contexts that make leaving poverty nearly impossible. When she was on her book tour, people asked her all kinds of inappropriate questions based on the assumptions they made about her as an unmarried, Black mother. "I had to say, 'Listen. I don't know what you're trying to do here, but that's not my narrative. I feel very empowered. I don't feel constrained by what society says. I wanted to be a mom, so I became a mom. That's it.'"

While she doesn't let what others might think of her get in her way, she's frustrated by the paucity of complex, nuanced stories about single moms. "I'm a single mom. I feel very fulfilled. I'm happy. I don't feel burdened. I don't feel haggard at the end of the day. I go out. I have fun. But those are not the stories. Frankly, I don't think anybody wants to hear those kinds of stories, of a happy single mom."

Nicole became a mom when she was thirty-four. "I'm going to start this big job at NYU. I don't have a partner. I'm single, a *Sex in the City* lady. I tell the woman I'm dating, 'Just so you know, I'm going to start trying to get pregnant in January.' This is, like, September. I say, 'You can either stay with me or you don't. This is what I'm going to do.' So she's like, 'Okay.' I don't think she believed me, really. January, I started the process. By February, I was pregnant."

6. C. Nicole Mason, *Born Bright: A Young Girl's Journey from Nothing to Something in America* (New York: St. Martin's Press, 2016).

Many of her friends initially wondered what the hell she was doing having kids without a partner when she had just started a new job. But they supported her through her pregnancy and then as community for her kids. "They have tons of aunties. People love them. They need a community. They need love. They need people who show up for them. People who see them. People who value them. That's all they care about. Some people feel like those kinds of relationships are more temporary or transient because they're not biologically tied. I would push back and say, 'I would say that about my own biological family.'"

After her babies were born, Nicole quickly turned her attention to getting back to work. "Because of the kind of pressure I put on myself, about my work, motherhood wasn't going to change that. I worked myself ragged. When I went back to NYU, I sort of pretended like I didn't have the kids. I was really compartmentalizing. I still worked long hours. It was maddening. I was able to sustain that craziness because I had this community who showed up for me. One time, I forgot I was traveling out of town until I got to work. I called a couple friends. I was like, 'Look. I fucked up. I have to go out of town right now. I need somebody to pick them up from school and then stay with them.' They were like, 'Okay.'"

As for so many of us, accepting and asking for help was hard for Nicole. "The biggest yes—and I think I've been growing ever since—was when my grandmother offered to come to help me with the kids when they were born. I initially told her no. I was like, 'I'll be fine.' I was like, 'Maybe you can come for like a week.' When she got here, I was like, 'Holy fuck.' First of all, I cannot afford the cost of childcare for two kids. Two, the way my life is set up . . . So, she ended up staying for eighteen months."

While Nicole is the first to point out that her income, education, and access to social capital all protect her and her kids from some of the very real challenges many single mothers face, she fiercely believes that we can access a significant amount of agency when it comes to how we construct family for ourselves. "Now, what it looks like for you, the little particulars and the granular stuff, that's up for debate. But is the life that you want to create, or family you want to create, available to you? Yes, if you are willing to throw off all this negative shit about what family is. If you can quiet that, it's all you."

What Nicole said about mind-set echoes much of what I heard from others. Whether it was about marriage or parenting or location, for many of us, it doesn't make sense to stick to the picture of family we came up with earlier in our lives. It might be that our desires change or that our circumstances just don't line up with an old vision. Either way, many people told me that discarding the picture they had of how their lives would be—sometimes joyfully, sometimes through grieving—was necessary in order to fully embrace something better, or at least accept something different.

THE COST OF COMMUNITY

The summer we moved into our house, my daughter, who was five at the time, discovered that two kids lived next door—Kaleela and her younger sister, Mercedes. Stella and Kaleela would play in our adjacent front yards and the collective protective eyes of our neighborhood turned toward the street and sidewalk because suddenly there were kids playing outside. The previously vacant and quiet tree-lined street was now occupied by little kids, inspiring our adult neighbors' vigilance and creating an opportunity to connect.

The sisters' mom, Elaine, became my sidewalk conversation buddy. We both worked from home, and I often found myself passing twenty or thirty minutes talking with her when I was heading into my house from my car. I loved having them as neighbors. I trusted Elaine with my kids because she is a thoughtful and aware parent. She also has the critical analysis of race that I'd want for a white woman raising mixed-race Black girls. She'd watch our kids if Nino or I needed to run quick errands. We'd have Mercedes for dinners and sleepovers.

Elaine's story is one that would be easy to judge and dismiss based on stereotypes. And she is the first to admit that when it comes to creating community, she struggles. Part of what I appreciate about her and the path she's taken so far is that it complicates what we so often disparagingly paraphrase about the lives of single women raising children in precarious financial circumstances.

In the beginning, her daughters' father was someone she'd gone on a few dates with and decided it wasn't going to work out. They weren't in touch when she found out she was pregnant, but she decided she was ready to become a mother. Several months later, she tracked him down and found out he was locked up in San Quentin, a California state prison. To Elaine's surprise, Darrick was happy about becoming a father. His enthusiasm fed into the idea they both entertained about getting back together and becoming a family.

At the time, Elaine was living rent-free in a house owned by a community of activists. "I didn't have credit. I couldn't get a loan, I didn't have any money to put down on it. And I was in school at the time. So, I paid a little bit of rent, but then after Kaleela was born, I didn't really have any income. So, I stayed there rent-free." While it was helpful to not have to pay rent, Elaine felt a bit like their charity project, something they could point at to feel good about themselves, when, in fact, they were well resourced and provided her with a basic human right she should have anyway.

When Darrick got out of prison the terms of his release required that he live at a halfway house, but he moved in with Elaine. The next couple of years had him on the run from the cops and in and out of jail, sometimes living with Elaine and Kaleela, sometimes living with his mother, sometimes living on the street.

"I held on to the idea that we could have a good relationship, live together, raise our kids together. I kind of held on to that for a while, even though it went back and forth, we were in and out of relationship, he was in and out of the house, he was in and out of jail."

She wanted another child and they got pregnant again. But Darrick was not doing well and Elaine decided to end things. With Darrick out of the picture, she shifted her idea of what family was going to be for her. "From that point on, I let go of all of my expectations of him. I decided, 'Okay, it's just me.' It made everything a lot easier in many ways. There was no one to resent for not doing what I thought they should do. And in that sense, when I compare myself to my friends who are fighting with their partners or husbands or whatever over whose responsibility is what, and how to make decisions and stuff, my life feels easier because there's no one to fight with, because I just let it all go."

With her own family in Wyoming, Elaine had to rely on girlfriends and Darrick's mother for some practical and emotional support. Elaine and her friends with children would exchange childcare, though it was mostly Elaine watching their kids. And her friends would sometimes help her out financially.

"One of my friends went to law school, and I watched her kids quite a bit while she was doing that. And another friend of mine, for a while her husband would drop their son off at my house in the morning and go to work, and then I would take all the kids to school." Part of the imbalance in childcare was circumstantial—Elaine was self-employed and worked at home, making it comparatively more practical for her to watch kids. But part of it was her own reluctance to ask for help because of that tired American Dream insistence on independence. "I am not good at asking for help. It's not where my mind goes first. It doesn't even occur to me. And if I remember that I should, then it's hard for me, it takes work to get around to it. I suppose it's just kind of ingrained in me that I should not need help. On an intellectual level that sounds ridiculous. I can think about it and say, 'Of course you can ask for help.' But I don't do it. I mean, everything from carrying a piece of furniture or something. I'll first try to do it myself."

For moms without partners, in addition to generally not having another set of hands in their home, they are burdened with society's chastisement and assumptions about their circumstances, especially if they access public benefits like food stamps or Section 8 housing vouchers. "I think one of the hardest things is the shame around receiving public assistance. Being on welfare, getting food stamps, all of that. And again, it's one of those things where, on an intellectual level, I know that it's justified, and I can make righteous claims that everyone should be paid: you should earn a living as a stay-at-home parent, and everyone has the right to housing. But the shame and stigma around it is really deeply ingrained. I don't tell people that I get food stamps. And I catch myself thinking things like, 'Why is it so hard for me? I see there's this other person who doesn't have to resort to this, and is making it work, and is surviving. And maybe I'm just lazy. I need to do something more, I need to work harder. I have a college degree, why aren't I earning enough of a living to have a house or whatever?' I catch myself thinking those things."

One winter, Elaine got sick with pneumonia. It made her feel that the life she and her kids had was more precarious than she was comfortable with. "It was a bit of a turning point for me. What if it had been something worse? I wanted to be closer to my family. I know that all the neighbors and my friends would totally have helped me out with the kids. But not in a long-term situation."

So, she and the girls moved to Wyoming, where Elaine's family lived. It's easier for them financially. Elaine was able to find housing she could afford with her work as a translator and transcriber. And, as she says, "Out here near my family, if there was a real long-term emergency, my kids could go live with someone."

The feeling of precariousness she was having has subsided now that she's geographically close to her parents. But it hasn't really been helpful for the day-to-day. They're a twenty-minute drive apart and her mother doesn't drive. Her mom has health issues and her dad works the swing shift— they're not super available.

Too, after a year and a half, Elaine hasn't really made friends. Culturally, she doesn't love where she lives. And whereas on our block in Oakland she could spend her day at home working but step outside to chat with whomever happened by on the sidewalk, now she's working in her apartment in an apartment complex and there's no one outside to have those unplanned but socially grounding conversations. She gained some much needed security, but lost community.

Part of what I find so clarifying about Elaine's story is that she was in this untenable situation, having to choose between community and family and financial stability. Whenever I hear economists talking about where jobs are with the assumption that people will move to those areas, I think about how they are ignoring what it means for people to uproot themselves from home to go someplace where they don't know anyone. They are underestimating the hardship caused by leaving community.

SIX

Make This Space for People, Make This Space for Me

Navigating Hardship

> She is a friend of my mind. She gather me, man.
> The pieces I am, she gather them and give them
> back to me in all the right order.[1]
>
> —TONI MORRISON

M Y FATHER, MAURICE Hope Thompson, was a renaissance man and master of the side hustle. He hosted a public affairs show on KTSU, the radio station at Texas Southern University (TSU), where he also taught students the ins and outs of broadcast journalism and the radio industry. He had a master's in journalism and a law degree. He was a runner his entire adult life, with no health vices other than a persistent sweet tooth. When I was a kid, we would make ice cream with one of those wooden ice-cream makers that required a steady supply of rock salt and hand cranking. He liked flavors I found much too unconventional, like pistachio and kiwi. He was also a photographer and rarely without his

---

1. Toni Morrison, *Beloved* (New York: Knopf, 2007), 321.

camera bag, spending weekends and evenings at weddings, parties, and events. The last conversation I had with my father was around the end of 2009. I was buying a new camera and wanted his advice.

My dad died in January 2010 when I was pregnant with my son. His death was unexpected. Even though he'd been diagnosed with cancer a few years before, he was doing well after a bone marrow transplant and clinical trials. Ultimately, what killed him was the drugs he was taking to manage the side effects of his treatment. But I was thankful that those same drugs allowed him to live as long as he did and that he knew before he died that he was going to have a second grandchild. I'm thankful he went quickly, going about his business.

As his only child and "next of kin," I received the call that he had died. I was sitting on my bed when my phone rang, opening a box that had just arrived—inside was the camera my dad had helped me choose. On the phone was my dad's longtime friend James Douglas, who also worked at TSU. My dad hadn't shown up for work the day before, so his colleagues went to his home to check on him. It was my responsibility to inform family, to decide what to do with his body (Who knows about what to do with a body?), sort through his things (my dad was an *impressive* hoarder), and plan his memorial. It was overwhelming to be in charge of all these things and to mourn at the same time—while pregnant. But my dad had so many people, and belonged to two enormous communities—his church and the university. With them and our family, I quickly realized that I was not going to be doing anything alone.

I flew to Texas. A few of his friends had cleaned his house enough for some of us to stay in. And my aunts—his sisters—my uncle, my cousins, my intrepid mother, and my mother-in-love all flew in to handle what we knew would be the daunting task of going through his things, and to plan and attend his memorial. We tackled the enormous mess and treasure chest that was his home (a 1987 receipt from Taco Bell in an unlabeled box stuck to a photo of my grandfather from the 1950s . . .). We filled dozens and dozens of industrial-strength, extra-large trash bags with decades of detritus and possibly irreplaceable valuables; gave away clothes, tools, and appliances; collected mementos (letters to his mother, a copper bracelet, his old-school pressure cooker). We planned the readings and songs for the memorial.

When there is shit to be done, I compartmentalize. I put my feelings down and take care of business. This was no different. My dad's three-bedroom plus two-car garage house was full of stuff with no organization. It was some of the realest shit I've ever faced. My family and my father's friends deferred to my leadership and stepped into theirs when I asked. I'm sure I was not my kindest, most thoughtful self. It sounds so clichéd to say, but truly their love and what is accurately described as devotion, to both me and my father, carried me. Everyone spent long hours cleaning and sorting. His friend Sheila handled collecting info about trash pickup, landlord contacts, and myriad other things so I didn't even have to think about it. My mother-in-love, who was also my midwife, made sure I ate and hydrated. My mom did exactly what I told her, like a champion. My aunts handled the details of the service. Somewhere in there, I wrote a eulogy.

There were two services—one at his church and one at TSU. It was an incredible gift to meet literally hundreds of people who loved my dad, and whom he loved, supported, and taught. There were so many young people who he was a father figure to. I think a lot of people who aren't raised by their dads might resent any fathering they give to other people. I credit my mother with making sure that I didn't lack for love and caring adults in my life so that I didn't miss my dad's semiabsence. My dad always wanted to have more kids and I'm glad he was able to play a parental role in so many other lives.

At the end of it all, my mother-in-love, Jacque, and I were the last ones to leave his house. I finished some last minute things, and abandoned others, as she waited in my dad's truck. It had started raining. I looked around to make sure I wasn't leaving anything behind, closed the door behind me, and collapsed, sobbing, on the little cement landing, gripping the cold metal railing to keep from falling over completely. Thinking back on it now, it reminds me of labor. There was a point during my son's birth when my contractions changed very suddenly from gripping to pushing. I was not in control; my body and the wisdom it held from thousands of years of evolution took over. My body did the same with my grief. It seized my bones and muscles and pushed it out. There in the rain outside my dad's home, I bawled and shook wildly for a few moments.

Jacque and I had canceled our return flights to California because I wanted to drive home in his truck with the stuff of his I wanted to keep and re-create a road trip he and I had taken when I was eighteen. During my winter break from college, we had driven from Houston to LA to visit his brother, my Uncle Peter, and Peter's wife, Yvonne. My dad loved to drive long distances. He would drive from Houston to Oberlin, Ohio, to visit me in college or from Houston to

Toronto to visit his sisters. For that trip to LA, we got into his black Nissan Z and basically drove 1,500 miles straight through. We did not stop to stay anywhere, we'd just take turns driving and napping. We stopped in New Mexico, where he bought a silver ring that I wear whenever I need him close. My dad, a very devout man, tried to have me read the Bible out loud to him when he was driving. I was supremely annoyed by this, and for once in my life thankful that reading in cars makes me nauseous.

We were on the road back to Houston for New Year's. I insisted that we stop somewhere before midnight so we could count down properly. We stopped at a for-real, middle-of-nowhere truck stop somewhere in Texas. I swear the music on the jukebox stopped when we walked into that diner full of white people who all turned and looked at us. My dad didn't give a shit. We had pie and grape juice (because grapes, wine, champagne) and toasted in 1993.

Jacque, because she is adventurous and supportive, was game for this pilgrimage—though for sure, we would be stopping along the way. We talked and talked on the drive. Jacque told me what she wants when she dies—to be buried in comfortable clothing with some good books. She also gave me the kind of advice you give your best friends.

My dad had life insurance that gave me enough money for a down payment on a house.[2] Nino and I had vague plans to

---

2. We moved into our house in the beginning of July of that year, about a week before my son was born. Solomon came into our lives two weeks before his due date (thank goodness; he was ten pounds) in a birthing tub at the foot of our bed. I caught him myself and then handed him to Jacque so she could give him a midwife's once-over and a grandma's embrace.

save some money to get an FHA loan to buy a house eventually. So, when I found out my dad had life insurance, I knew exactly what I would do with it. On that trip home, Jacque told me to make sure that I set it up so that if Nino and I ever split up, I'd get my money back. So I did, and I'm not sure it would have occurred to me if she hadn't bought it up. (Nino loves that his mom and I are so close, though I think he thinks I get a little too much glee out of that story.)

From Houston to Oakland, I cycled through sweet nostalgia, reflection, gripping loss, overwrought euphoria, and panic. Jacque claimed the job of taking care of the in-process baby in my mourning body. She kept me well fed, hydrated, and rested. She also witnessed and protected my grief.

We had a bunch of stuff strapped to the top of my dad's truck. One evening a rainstorm came in and I wrapped all the stuff on the roof in plastic trash bags and strapped it down. A kind and reasonable man came by and, looking at the obviously pregnant woman balanced precariously on the open backseat door and wrestling with rope in the rain, asked Jacque, "Does she need help?" Jacque told him no. She knew that this absurd task was part of my process, that I needed to do it myself.

The ability to hold space for another's experience is a critical one. It's not about giving advice or trying to fix anything, but witnessing and just being an active, attentive presence. Sitting with the grief and pain of other people can be so hard. I often find it uncomfortable to just listen and watch a loved one in distress. I want to fix, I want to advise. I had to read parenting books to learn about holding my children's physical and emotional pain. And I still get it wrong. With my kids and my friends, I'm working on just saying, "I'm sorry that happened to you" or "That sounds hard" or "Whatever you're feeling is okay," or not saying anything and just listening or sitting in silence. I'm trying to be better at clarifying what would be helpful—Do you want me to listen or would some advice be helpful?—but I still struggle with it.

I want to believe it's because I love them so much that I don't want them to suffer. That's partly true, but it's also that empathy can be uncomfortable. So, my efforts to soothe are partly about not having to feel bad alongside someone else. I'm learning to step back enough to make it not about me.

Too, expressing pain is seen as weakness; and in a culture that despises weakness, we don't have much public modeling for how to support one another as we inevitably experience rejection, heartbreak, disappointment, and loss. Around death, we are especially silent and so much of the process is invisible.

When Lennon Flowers was a senior in college, her mother died from lung cancer. Meeting people became fraught; she worried they'd ask what her parents did and she'd have to talk about her mother's death. She worried that she'd make people uncomfortable and felt that her life was too much for others to handle.

So, she compartmentalized, putting aside her grief and heartache to focus on being a good student. Not having peers who could relate to her story isolated her grief. Years later, she moved to LA and met Carla, whose father had recently died. A few months later, she and Carla had a dinner with other women who'd lost a parent. Soon, they were having monthly dinners. Their table grew into an organization called the Dinner Party and specifically serves people in their twenties and thirties, who are likely to be the first among their friends to experience the death of a significant loved one.

The Dinner Party has maintained its informal approach—it's not therapy or a traditional grief support group run by a professional—and shares some similarities to Alcoholics Anonymous in that way. There is a broad structure, but anyone can plug into the network of hosts or attend a gathering with the intention of building community with others who understand something that profoundly impacts your life. There are some who are drawn to it because no one they know shares their experience. Others may have surviving family members, but as Lennon explained to me, it's not always your family who knows you best or with whom you can share and process your grief.

Aisha found out about the Dinner Party through a bereavement group at Columbia University, where she was in graduate school. Aisha grew up in Harlem, raised by her mother. Many of her mom's friends played a significant role in her life practically—like picking her up from school—and as role models. One woman, Victoria, whom she thinks of as a godmother, was Buddhist and taught Aisha how to meditate. "I went around and had adventures with her, meeting Buddhist monks and going to mediation camps as a young child." This was part of Aisha's eclectic spiritual upbringing. While Sunday was for church, she also got palm readings, tarot card readings, and Reiki.

Aisha's father was a part of her life—providing financial support and showing up for events like birthdays and graduations—but an infrequent presence. She reconnected with him when she was in college, living with him for a period of time. After graduation, Aisha moved to China to teach English. Meanwhile, her father, who'd had heart trouble in the past, was experiencing recurring health issues. He kept the seriousness of his illness from her. Meanwhile, Aisha got into a graduate program at Columbia and was getting ready to move back to New York. "We would talk on the phone. He was like, 'You just keep doing good in school. School is important. I'll be fine; don't worry about me.' But he wasn't telling me how dire the situation was." It was one of her sisters who told her how sick he was. He died in the hospital on New Year's Day, during Aisha's first year of grad school.

The first Dinner Party she attended, right after her dad died, was powerful and she built immediate kinship with others at the table. But the host never reached out to the group again and Aisha was devastated by the emotional whiplash of feeling alone, then connected, then alone again so soon after her father's death. But she was placed in another group and began attending dinners every month or so.

"My only issue was I was always the only Black person at the table. I had to deal with racism, I'd had to deal with horrible things with doctors. And a lot of people in my group didn't understand that. Because they'd be like, 'Oh, I had a horrible experience with a doctor.' But I'm like, 'Yeah, but your horrible experience and my horrible experience is not the same thing. Doctors would talk down to me, talk down to my dad—like we're idiots.'"

Aisha decided she would host her own table just for people of color, so she went through the Dinner Party's training. During a lot of back-and-forth with them about what constituted diversity ("What white people think and what I think are two different things"), Aisha broke her foot and had to put her plans on pause. When she recovered enough to move around, she decided she wanted to try again. This time when she reached out, they welcomed the idea of her hosting a table for people of color.

Aisha is very passionate about her table and her role in pioneering a people of color Dinner Party group in New York. She is fierce about making sure that the environment is safe and everyone feels taken care of. "People think, 'I'm ready to meet people, maybe make some friends, talk about grief.' And then they get scared." She makes sure there's food for everyone even though it's a potluck ("Everybody got an allergy. I know everybody's allergies; I write it down on my spreadsheet"). She organizes how many mains, sides, and salads there will be to make sure people get a real meal ("I would bring food and maybe one other person would bring food; but everybody else was bringing wine and cookies"). She coordinates with everyone's schedules ("I send out Doodles,[3] Doodles with fifteen different dates, and see which one is the most popular").

She talked with her roommates to set clear expectations about what was required when she was hosting. "You can't be running up and down the stairs while someone is telling us that their brother committed suicide. They're either not in the house or they stay in their room. Because they know they don't wanna hear from me. Because I'm gonna be like, 'Look, you knew what it was being my roommate. You knew this was something that's important to me. You can give me two hours on a Sunday to make this environment. And make this space for people. And make this space for me.'"

---

3. Doodle.com is an online meeting coordination tool.

Through all this care—putting together an environment conducive to people building trust and opening up about what is likely the most painful experience of their lives, not to mention her persistence in getting the group started in the first place—she is engaging in that doing-for-others-is-doing-for-yourself work. So often, the thing we're missing in our lives is something others are missing as well. Some people launch organizations to make the thing they need; others gather a few friends. This is what it looks like to ask for and offer help, to build relationships that can hold us accountable to ourselves, to open up to knowing others and letting ourselves be known.

"IT WOULD HAVE BEEN SOONER, BUT MY WIFE DIED."

It is obvious to you by now that the stories I've shared with you primarily feature people of color who are women, transgender men, and gender-nonconforming people. But I did interview several cis men, mostly white, about their experience of community and family. Many of them felt that while they were socialized to America's dominant culture of masculinity—what the Oakland Men's Project and educator Tony Porter call the Man Box[4]—they recognized how confining it is and are working to redefine masculinity for themselves. They were also clear that the socialization they received was deep and undoing it would be a lifelong journey.

---

4. Mark Greene, "The History of 'The Man Box,'" Medium, January 15, 2019, https://medium.com/@remakingmanhood/the-history-of-the-man-box-e6eed6d895c4.

My friend Adam (white, cis, straight) told me that he
feels like his generation of men (he's a Gen Xer, like me)
is really grappling with how to be available and emotionally
connected, really redefining for themselves what it means to
be men and looking for models to guide them. My friend
Anthony ("ethnically ambiguous" white and Mexican, cis,
straight) talked to me about the challenges of raising his son
to be both a whole, deeply feeling, caring person and prepared for a society that still insist that boys don't cry, show
vulnerability, or need other people.

"There's stuff that I do to try to keep him tender," Anthony told me. "I hug him a lot, and give him kisses, and
cuddle him, and just try to make that affection feel normal."
But his own socialization makes him worry about his son being protected as well.

"When I was growing up, you couldn't be tender; that was
not a safe option. This is both a function of masculinity as
it's performed in our society, as well as the kind of neighbor-
hoods and circumstances I grew up in." One of the limitations
of it is the exhaustion of having to have your guard up. "It's
like having to put on armor. I guess that's the best metaphor
that I could use. And I really do mean that metaphor very
intentionally. Because it isn't just the protective shield, but
it also makes it harder for you to move around in the world.
And it's heavy, it's a burden. I've worked really hard in my
adulthood to (a) kind of drop some of that shit; but (b) make
sure that I'm in circumstances where I don't have to wear it in
the first place. But it's fucking exhausting. And it's painful."
This shouldn't be misunderstood as the I-have-it-so-hard-as-
a-man backlash we see anytime men are called on their privilege or their abusive sexism and misogyny. Anthony speaks

clearly to the way that patriarchy hollows the humanity out of men.

Several men told me that some of their hardest growth is around the vulnerability required to navigate hardship. When they are having a hard time in their lives is when it's the hardest to reach out for, or accept, support. This really hit home for me during two unexpected conversations I had a couple summers ago.

I was talking to Sean on the phone because he was the creator and proprietor of a device I use for my chickens, and I was complaining about a faulty piece of his product. He promised to send me an improved replacement part. He also let me know that he'd redesigned the whole product and would be releasing the new version in the fall. Then he said, "It would have been sooner, but my wife died." At this moment, I could have expressed my condolences and wrapped up the phone call.

Maybe it was his engaged approach to customer service. Maybe it was just that I like hearing people's stories. Whatever it was, something encouraged me to stay on the phone and listen. Sean and I spent another thirty minutes on the phone. He told me about his wife's sudden death, about how terribly (understandably) his teenage children were managing it—substance abuse, obsessive-compulsive disorder—how therapy had barely held any of them together, how for the first time in a year, he hadn't woken up sobbing. All of this deeply personal suffering poured out of him and I mostly listened, offering the occasional affirmation. What struck me about his experience, other than the obvious devastation of losing a loved one, was how alone he was in his grief. I know grief is a lonely experience, but his wife was clearly his major social support and connection. He did not have the kind of friends and community who were really present to care for him and his kids.

Later that summer, I spent a few days at a friend's house in the Santa Cruz Mountains. I was there alone and one of the pipes burst. The local handyman, Oren, came by to try to fix it. Oren is probably in his seventies. He's a white man who wears overalls and walks with a cane, moving slowly and with deliberation. He can fix anything. He's also a talker. After he looked at the pipes, he joined me on the porch where I was reading. He proceeded to talk with (at, really) me about the "turd door" at the Kings Canyon sewage treatment plant, being a boat skipper, ruining his knees tiling floors, and the woman with the Marilyn Monroe skull tattoo who came to his house to help care for his dying wife.

He spent the most time talking about his wife—how he drove her to medical appointments, advocated for her with doctors, tried to get her to eat, her good days and bad days. Oren choked up more than once talking about her. It was clear to me that, like Sean, he did not have much social support outside his wife and he would be devastatingly lonely when she died.

The way Sean and Oren told me, a complete stranger, about their pain from loss was revealing. Neither of them has community supporting them. Neither of them has close friends encircling them in love and care. Grief is a wreckage. And in so many ways, it is something we experience utterly alone. But without the company of loved ones, our path toward reclaiming life and healing in the midst of grief, or any hardship, is perilously hindered.

"WE HAVE TO MAKE SURE THAT
WE'RE ALL ALL RIGHT."

While I've experienced the grief that comes from the death of loved ones, witnessing the illness and death of Alana Devich Cyril and the grief of her partner, Malkia "Mac" Devich Cyril, has helped me understand my own grief more deeply, and continues to teach me what it means to support someone else through hardship.

But I have to start with the love. Mac and Alana gave their broader community the gift of their story of falling in love and their epic wedding—Love's Revival—through social media. I was among hundreds of others who delighted in the snippets of "Mitts and Muffy's" conversations that showed up in my news feed.

> MAC: Why would you get me fancy, dark chocolate peanut butter cups? You know I prefer regular Reese's.
> ALANA: I got them for myself. They're my favorite.
> MAC: Oh. My bad. Also, I ate them.

The love story of Alana and her "studsband" is a life-affirming, joyful, honest, beautiful, real-life homage to what's possible when two souls find their truth and resonance with each other. They are beloved among their very broad community. When Alana was diagnosed with stage IV gastro-esophageal cancer, they asked that same community for help. They needed help covering tens of thousands of dollars in medical bills, and they needed help making their home more accessible as Alana became less mobile. They asked for myths and memes and funny videos to bring them more laughter. They asked for aromatherapy, cannabis, massages, and salves to ease the debilitating physical and emotional pain they both experienced. They asked for our prayers, our best wishes, our belief in miracles. And we gave it to them. I didn't know Mac or Alana well, but when I saw a request I could fulfill, I jumped at the opportunity.

And when Alana died in October 2018, Mac and their closest family asked for quotes, anecdotes, and favorite songs to celebrate Alana's brilliance, humor, and vibrancy. Her homegoing was a beautiful celebration of joy, love, and laughter. And it is community that continues to be with and witness Mac as they grieve and try to find a way forward.

Like many of the folks who have provided company and resources, and lit candles, I've been honored to do my little part in supporting them. It feels purposeful. Too, I've learned from watching the people closest to them what showing up demands—careful tending, bravery, arms long and strong enough to make a container for bottomless sorrow. I'm sure it's something many learn just by doing it, and I'm in awe of love like that.

Hardship is very clarifying. It distills the relationships that can withstand real life. It shows us who will show up and how. It's the people who don't run away when shit gets real who can be our kin.

Angela had mixed feelings when she found out she was pregnant. But about five months in, Angela began to really connect with the baby and the idea of being a mother to this new person. While she was afraid she and her daughter wouldn't bond when she was born, she experienced the immediate recognition and attachment that often happens with mothers and their newborns. But during this period of focused attention on pregnancy and then motherhood, her partner became increasingly abusive—verbally and sometimes physically. At this point, Angela was financially dependent on him. Even when she went back to work full time, she wasn't making enough to support her and Isabella on her own.

Like many women who experience abuse, the fear and shame she felt kept her from talking to her friends about what was going on, so she tackled it on her own.

"Things were bad enough about a year into it that I knew I needed to get serious about my career, so that I could leave eventually. I took a leap and took a director's job. I remember this being an actual concrete thought in my mind: 'I need to take this job because I need to be able to leave him pretty soon.'" Even though the job wasn't a good fit, she stayed there a year so she could begin to get back on solid financial ground. Then, she found a job that would change everything.

"I remember my first day of work. That morning, he threw a hot cup of coffee in my face. I remembered having to go in with the smell of coffee in my hair and be introduced to everyone. And of course everybody is like, 'Oh! You have a partner and a kid!' And you have to sit there and smile. I remember smelling the coffee and just smiling. I remember thinking to myself, 'I'm going to bust my ass here so that I can move up as quickly as possible so that I can get the fuck out of this relationship.'"

She'd been hiding the abuse for years—covering bruises or saying she fell off her bike. "I had to change my contact lenses all the time, because I cried so much. My eyes were always puffy, and I'd say I'd had an allergy attack." But three months after she started her new job, her partner kicked her so badly that she couldn't sit for weeks. The next morning she told Julie, one of her best friends, what was going on and dropped Isabella off at Julie's house. She cashed out her 401(k), and four days later she had a sublet for her daughter and herself.

During this transition crisis, she finally began to tell people in her life what had been going on—including telling her new boss, who helped her secure permanent housing. "I really did start building a different foundation of meaningful relationships with people. I was lucky to have some good people in my life already, but it deepened at that point, when I knew I was going to leave Isabella's dad."

The struggle of asking for help is amplified when the society you live in already judges you as a failure. Angela, like many of the single mothers I talked with, feels like she has to prove that she can do it all on her own. "I'm very caught up in having my shit together and doing so much. I need to look together. I don't want to look like the crazy person I feel like in my brain a lot. I know it's about self-worth and self-value. I see where I've let it go and I see where it really still hangs on."

Sage Crump recognizes the ways in which American Dreamism tells us to be independent and demonstrate strength by doing it ourselves, so she is working on it for herself and others. "Showing up for people I love in my life is a really core value for me. That's where the work is—being so present, being aware, and looking for where you can support, so people don't have to ask you. Because, you know, asking is hard. We're already battling so many different ways we are told we are not enough. We are so practiced in this idea of self-reliance." Like Caroline from Chapter 5, Sage thinks it can be really important to give help without being asked. "I feel like showing up for folks, like 90 percent of it, is proactive. Because the majority of asks will never happen. And you find out later that folks didn't have any food. Or you find out later their water has been off. And you're like, what? And I know for me, I get hurt. I'm tearing up right now because that hurts me. Someone I love is going without and didn't ask me. I don't want you to have to live like that. If there's anything I can do, even if it's just, here's my gym membership card, go shower whenever you want to. Whatever resources we have to make sure that we're all all right."

In Angela's case, it was both logistics, like drop-off and pickup or changing diapers, and emotional support so she could process her trauma. "That first couple of years was really hard and scary, and I would be just sitting on people's couches finally able to tell the story of it, finally coming clean and being real with all the shit that I used to hide."

And sometimes it was about being available to Isabella. "My primary, core, female friends who have really been there for me—they're all aunties. They all keep up on the day-to-day with me. And for Isabella, they provide a real mutual comfort. They'll just talk to her and tell her what to do in front of me. They don't have to ask, 'Is it okay if she does this?' They're just like, 'No, get over there. What are you doing? Sit down. Go be nice to your mom.'"

OUR UNDENIABLE INTERDEPENDENCE

Jenna thought she'd found someone truly remarkable with whom she could safely have a relationship that reflected her radical gender politics. She and Malcom were both involved in racial and gender justice advocacy and research. They fell in love and moved in together. They committed to having an open relationship. "It was really based on some radical queer politics shit. We read books about open relationships and polyamory, we read all the guides. We had all these honest conversations and we drafted a relationship contract."

But Malcom was not honest—with himself or Jenna—about how insecure their arrangement made him. Their relationship deteriorated and they broke up. Malcom is a dad who has joint custody of his kids, who spent every other weekend with him and Jenna. Rather than uproot Malcom and his kids, Jenna moved out.

Moving during winter in Jenna's East Coast college town is particularly challenging since there are few vacancies. It's also expensive no matter the time of year, because most leases require first and last months' rent, a security deposit, not to mention a broker's fee—the equivalent of four months' rent. Jenna found a temporary situation and borrowed money from friends so she could move. She was relieved to have a relatively quick transition as she geared up to submit her tenure dossier while handling a full teaching load.

But when Jenna complained to her new landlord, Woody, that the front door didn't lock, he said, "Well, that door's been there for five years, and no one's ever complained about it before." A month after she moved in, the apartment flooded from above. She also discovered that the electrical work in parts of her apartment were ungrounded. She brought all of it up with Woody. Woody, it turns out, was a total asshole.

"I'm a fairly resilient person. If I have a plan and feel like I can make the plan happen, I feel empowered. So, when the breakup happened, it really sucked. But I felt fine because I was like, 'Okay, I have a plan of escape and I'm going to move.' But then when I moved into this disaster place and all this other stuff started happening, it really did feel like it was out of my control. Every time I would try to regain control of the situation, the landlord would do crazy, crazy shit. There were no rules of behavior." When Jenna said she would report him to the department of housing, he threatened her.

Jenna felt trapped because she didn't have the resources to leave. She'd already borrowed money from friends to move. "People loaned me large amounts of money. Then, I gave this dude the money and then it was gone, and I was living in this kind of hellhole."

She thought that maybe if she followed through on taking legal action, he would back off and she could get her money back and move out. So, she got a lawyer who served him with a demand letter telling him to give Jenna her money back.

The day her landlord was served, Jenna was sexually assaulted on her street. A stranger grabbed and groped her as she walked home in the middle of the day. The psychological and physical toll was overwhelming. The fear and anxiety was relentless. While her friends didn't doubt what Jenna was experiencing, they couldn't quite comprehend how terrible the situation was, which left her feeling isolated and detached. "It sounds dramatic, but there was definitely a point where I felt like my life was over. I felt like I had been financially destroyed, and that I wasn't going to be able to get back on my feet financially, and also I felt like I couldn't escape the unsafe situation, because of the financial thing."

And because Jenna is a scholar of political systems of oppression, her anger was more than personal. "I was also really,

really angry because I'm a person of relative privilege, and if this is how hard it is for me to survive being housing insecure, or having a shitty landlord, or having any of these bad series of events happen back to back, this is why there's so many women who are homeless. I cannot imagine . . . what if I had a child?"

Jenna stopped sleeping in her apartment and stayed with friends as much as possible. When she had to sleep in the apartment, she had male friends stay with her. "It was so sweet and I'll love them forever for doing that, but also I was extremely angry that I needed men to come sleep in my house in order for me to feel safe." During one of these security sleepovers, one of her friends got to witness, and ultimately intervene, during an encounter with her landlord. Someone else finally got to see how horrific the harassment was.

For some of us, our best experiences of family, love, and safety are associated with home. Anyone who has had the sanctity and safety of home taken away from them has been traumatized. Not having it, or the threat of not having it, is emotionally terrorizing.

Jenna's lawyer reassured her that she had an open-and-shut case and she should just keep documenting everything. But then they discovered that the landlord had been sued by three tenants previously and within months, all three times, he'd filed for bankruptcy. The lawyer was furious, but Jenna was distraught. And while her lawyer was willing to work on the case as long as it took, Jenna didn't have the money to pay him.

Harriet, a colleague of Jenna's, reached out. "I got a message from her that said, 'Hey, I don't know where things currently are. Hopefully you were able to get things resolved and you don't need this, but these people at my church just had a sudden death in the family, and are going out to Colorado for the summer. They need somebody trustworthy to take care of their house and mow their lawn and bring their mail in. Do you want me to connect you?'"

Jenna met with the couple once and they immediately agreed to have her stay in their house, rent-free, so she could get back on her feet and they didn't have to worry about an empty house. "All of a sudden, I went from feeling like there was no hope at all to being like, 'Oh my gosh, everything is going to be okay.'"

A few days later, her best friends arrived to help (coming from Washington and Minnesota), and another group of folks showed up, and in two days they packed up her entire apartment, moved her stuff into another friend's basement, and moved her to her temporary home.

"Their house was adorable. There was a fenced yard, so my dog could just go outside. There was a claw-foot bathtub, and the first time I took a bath, I felt like the whole world was new. Within the first two weeks of being at that house, I got my tenure dossier submitted. I applied for a raise. I got all this stuff done—it was literally all I needed. All I needed was a safe place, and I was able to get myself back on track. These strangers letting me live in their house, and I don't say this lightly, it renewed my faith in humanity."

As someone who prides herself on being able to handle her business, she felt awful asking for so much financial, practical, and emotional support. "I've learned and grown a lot about asking for help. Before all this happened, and trust me, I wish it hadn't happened, but I really wasn't good at asking for help, or accepting things from people in my life. I think I'm a lot better at it now, because I couldn't survive without it."

After the summer and another house-sitting gig, Jenna got an apartment in the same building as a friend. She also got two prestigious fellowships and tenure. And her friends celebrated her successes just as much as they supported her through crisis. The week her tenure letter arrived, she got taken out almost every night. A few months later, she planned a tenure/housewarming party. Some older, also single, women in academia gave her advice about the importance of celebrating milestones, outside of the traditional weddings and baby showers. They explained that there are ways single, child-free women get financially punished in a culture that celebrates marriage and motherhood.

So, Jenna created a registry, one that included the option of donating to activist organizations she cared about. She invited a few dozen people and made clear that presents were not the point. But her friends were eager to celebrate her by gifting her with things she would find useful. "It was so sweet, because people bought me things like sheets and towels and a comforter. I've never had a comforter in my entire life."

"I actually feel like my network is bigger now. My network's the same, but I didn't have the perception that all these people were a part of my network until I realized that they would show up for me in an emergency situation. I was really amazed that when I did start asking for help, there were people who I wouldn't have said were my friends who were totally the people I could go to for help in an emergency. It made me feel like I had more friends than I realized."

Hardships—big and small—and our need for help and support were woven through so many of the conversations I had for this book. Having people to share our joy, celebrate, or build something generative with is important. There is a reason holidays, birthdays, promotions, graduations, and births are marked with gatherings of others. But the reality of our undeniable interdependence really shows up when we struggle.

So much of our reluctance to ask for help is fear of being too much for others to handle and fear of the subsequent rejection we'd feel if others can't handle us. I've been thinking about the relationships I have where I end up feeling like I'm too much. In them, I retreat when I am feeling vulnerable. That is sometimes a reminder that vulnerability scares me and I may need to lean in and open up. But it is often information for me about what place those relationships can have in my life, and how much, and what kind of, energy I should give to them. I might really like those people, but maybe they are best thought of as what my friend Laurenellen calls "adventure buddies": people who will go do fun, interesting, enjoyable things with you (which could include watching a movie on the couch; it doesn't actually have to be an adventure). The people with whom I need to build more are the ones who can stomach my tears and falling apart and don't think I'm too much.

SEVEN

A Gathering and a Calling Home

The Remedies Are in Our Kitchens

Food is where we meet, where we build, where we
struggle, and where we survive.
—PEOPLE'S KITCHEN COLLECTIVE

M Y FAMILY IS not religious, but when we eat dinner together, we give thanks. We include the rain, the sun,
the moon, the soil, and the wind. Our gratitude starts with
"Thank you to all the hands that touched this food on its way
to our table." It's meant to acknowledge not just my husband
or me, who cooked the meal, but everyone from the farm
to the grocery store to our home who grew, harvested, fed,
slaughtered, transported, stocked, and bagged the food in our
meal. It's meant to acknowledge that it takes a lot of labor
from many, many people for us to eat. It's meant to make
visible the people we are connected to through our meal.

It is this thinking, writ large, that is foundational to the
work of the People's Kitchen Collective (PKC), an organization based in Oakland, California. I became aware of its work
several years ago through my friendship with Saqib Keval,
one of the founding members. Saqib, along with Jocelyn
Jackson and Sita Kuratomi Bhaumik, created PKC to "fill

our stomachs, but also nourish our souls, feed our minds, and fuel a movement."

PKC collaborates with chefs, activists, movement organizations, poets, performers, and everyday people to create events that center the experiences, social movements, and food of people of color. PKC creates beauty and nourishment that rejects the idea that the table is a place to avoid politics because, as Jocelyn said, "When you're at the table, everything at that table is political." Who grew, transported, and prepared the food speaks to labor and migration. What recipe is used speaks to cultural expression and history. Which ingredients are in the food points toward land use and the environment.

PKC makes these connections clear at its events, not just with the inclusion of speakers and performers who are talking about social justice issues, but with the inclusion of story and lineage behind everything from the location to the table decorations.

Their first event in the Bay Area took place in 2010 at a restaurant in San Francisco's Mission neighborhood and was focused on the gentrification that was occurring in that community. The menu was designed by a diversity of young people and elders from the neighborhood. One hundred and fifty families from the community were served at the pay-what-you-can six-course meal.

PKC does not think small. One hundred and fifty families is par for the course from this organization that largely relies on volunteers to prep, cook, serve, and clean up after its community meals.

The first PKC event I went to was in 2013 at Oakland's Life Is Living Festival, which brings together art, environmental justice, and community building. Every year, PKC makes and serves a meal modeled after the Black Panthers' free breakfast program. I showed up with my kids, who were three and eight at the time. It was a glorious day. Bobby Hutton Park was full of people of all ages. Throughout the day, there was a skateboarding competition, a mural installation, a graffiti battle, health screenings, music performances, a petting zoo, and a food justice symposium. But before all that, there was breakfast. I wasn't sure what to expect and, honestly, I don't recall what exactly we ate. But I do remember being worried that with hundreds of people to serve, it would take more time than my three-year-old was likely to sit still for. But it was so efficient, and the servers (who I now know were volunteers) were particularly caring and welcoming.

A few years passed before I experienced a PKC event again.

I was at a three-day training for a program I was taking, and our lunches were provided by People's Kitchen Collective. We were all chatting as we walked into the room where we'd eat.

Singing lifted above the din of our chatter.

"We who believe in freedom cannot rest!"

We all quieted down and listened to this tall Black woman with a beautiful, grounded voice sing to us. Jocelyn introduced herself and explained that in her family, the blessing before a meal was always sung. She told us a bit about PKC and the food we were about to enjoy. Unlike at most catered events, neither Jocelyn nor the food was invisible or in the background. She was not quietly bringing something to our experience; she created a table that she invited us to sit at. I remember feeling like a welcome guest in someone's home.

That feeling of home is exactly what Jocelyn comes from. She grew up in Kansas surrounded by extended family. "Oh my goodness, if I didn't have my family, I just don't even know what kind of person I would be. I got all the messages of how to be happy, of how to be on purpose, and to have agency, and responsibility, and self-determination."

Now Jocelyn splits her time between Las Vegas, where she helps raise her nephews, and the San Francisco Bay Area, where she combines food, art, and movement building with her partners at PKC and her own Justus Kitchen, a business that combines her love of food, community, and the environment.

The song she sings before a meal is a blessing, an acknowledgment of the food at the table, and also of all that comes before that—immediately and historically. "It's that power of connection, of 'this meal is a sacred moment.' It is something that brings together a moment that is filled with love, and it's also filled with healing," she told me. "It's the preparation for the food, being with my grandma and snapping peas, and learning all about her peach cobbler and lemon meringue recipes. And how she folded her dinner rolls in her palm in just a specific way. And cleaning collard greens. And figuring out that, really, people do eat possum and crow. And even though I don't like chitlins, I'm going to eat them because if I don't, something bad will happen."

The stories told, the time spent together, the learning and repeating tradition in the form of recipes or cooking practices is the path to each meal's meaning. "It leads up to this moment, this opportunity for family to join together in a circle and share breath, and also make harmony together. And that is all the metaphor I need in life!"

It took Jocelyn years to formally choose food as her conduit for community building and movement making. She left Kansas at eighteen and got a BA in fine arts. Then, she went to law school and practiced law in Washington, DC, for six years. After that were two years in Mali as a Peace Corps volunteer, then a master's in environmental education. "All the while I was trying to find out what this through-point is. I was trying to cobble it together, because there was something missing."

It all became clear to her on her thirty-eighth birthday. A friend organized a potluck to celebrate and insisted that Jocelyn do nothing but provide a list of names. "And I came to this gathering, and of course there's a sharing circle that happens, because that's just what happens—I'm a circle person. And in that circle, as people were giving me blessings and reflections, the refrain was food. The refrain was, 'Oh my god, I remember that thing that you cooked for me.'" For the first time, Jocelyn realized that making and sharing food was essential to who she is and what she wants to create in the world. "It wasn't ancillary, it's central. And it's central because it generates beloved community."

And it wasn't just that she recognized that food was her medium for creativity and purpose, but that her community recognized it as well.

THE OPPORTUNITY TO STICK OUR HAND IN SOMETHING AND PARTICIPATE

Sita also came to food through family and community. Sita is the child of immigrant parents—Indian on her father's side, and Japanese by way of Colombia on her mother's side. On both sides, Sita had aunts who held it down in the kitchen. Sita wanted two things: to connect with these women whose languages she did not speak and to bring the flavors of her parents' heritage to her own life in California. So, she began photographing her aunts in the kitchen, capturing them and their recipes, and brought them to her own kitchen.

Sita's community in California is an activist community. In her twenties, she was part of a leftist soccer league (despite not playing soccer). One Monday after a game, she had some of the players over because she'd made too much moussaka. It happened again the next week, and after three weeks there were forty people showing up at her house and she'd cook for them.

At the time, Sita was a board member for Kearney Street Workshop, the oldest Asian–Pacific American multidisciplinary arts organization in the United States. Each board member was responsible for raising one thousand dollars. Sita didn't have that much money or know anyone who did, but she knew how to cook and could do the math. "I had a fifty-person meal in my house. I cooked out of my oven, dropped a pizza on the floor, dusted it off. You know, the whole thing."

From meal kit services like Blue Apron and HelloFresh (which she refers to as the "white supremacy of food") to the way in which kitchens are hidden from restaurant patrons, Sita makes clear that we lose an opportunity when we are separated from the labor that happens before we lift a fork to our mouth.

"Your auntie is like the polar opposite of a restaurant in that she is like, 'I did this toiling away for eight hours making this for you!' Or when we have the opportunity to stick our hand in something and participate. We see that somebody's putting a lot of care into food.

"I think the reason there's such good juicy kitchen gossip, and so much connection happens in the kitchen, is because you are usually kind of doing something repetitive, and that releases something in your mind that creates a space that doesn't just reside in the brain, but also is something that becomes part of the body. And how often do we do that with each other?"

Part of what Sita is getting at is that the shared experience of preparing a meal, or even being in the kitchen while a meal is being prepared, is the kind of connection that reminds us to see and care about people.

"I think about how easy it is to go on Yelp and say, 'Oh, this food was bland, I did not like this restaurant.' But if you stand next to the person who's preparing it and you help them prepare it, and you know, maybe it is under seasoned. You're not going to say to their face like, 'I'm never coming back here.' You're going to say, 'Oh, can I have some salt? I like it a little on the salty side.' When you remove that link and it becomes about a service, people forget how to be kind to each other."

It's the making of harmony that Jocelyn talks about. The recipe choosing, ingredient selection, chopping, cooking, and serving that leads us to eating is all opportunity to build toward nourishment of the body *and* the spirit that builds togetherness.

COME AS YOU ARE

While People's Kitchen Collective engages on a large scale, I've learned from Saqib, Jocelyn, and Sita that the opportunity for togetherness, which was inspired by their homes, is something I wanted more of.

Nino and I occasionally have parties or gatherings in our house. It's a sweet home with a typical Craftsman layout. Even though the living room and dining room are fairly spacious and open, gatherings inevitably end up with a bunch of us crammed in the kitchen—leaning against the counters or sitting on our single red stool. The conversation is like a murmur of birds—sometimes the whole group swirls around a topic, then it will split into two or three smaller conversations, then come back together.

Our most regular party is an annual gathering called Soup & Pie that takes place the Saturday after Thanksgiving. Thanksgiving seems to put many of us in the mood for coming together, whether it's celebrating the national holiday or recognizing the genocide and continued racism experienced by Indigenous people. Soup & Pie allows us to circle up with community to continue that spirit of connection. We set it up as a potluck to which people can bring their leftovers. We provide both homemade soup (turkey and vegetarian) and pie (from our neighborhood favorite, Lois the Pie Queen), and our guests bring more of the same or something different. Every year I am filled with the satisfying warmth that comes from having so many loved ones gathered in my home. I also experience the low-key anxiety of hosting: cooking, mingling, introducing, managing, herding (kids), greeting, and the talking. I love it and wanted more of the satisfying warmth. But I wanted it without the hosting stress.

This desire had me thinking about the almost mythical practice of "dropping by." In my mind, it only occurred in small towns and ended decades ago. I can't imagine regularly showing up at friends' doors unannounced, expecting to be welcomed in and offered tea or wine, and to spend time catching up. But some evenings as I'm making dinner for my kids or we're all individually puttering around, I would welcome a friend or two stopping by so I could hug them and catch up. I also know that on other evenings, I want no part of anyone and enjoy the relative aloneness that I have in the company of Nino and our kids.

As you read in Chapter 5, this idea of dropping by came up in a conversation I had with Naomi. I asked her what family and community would look like in her ideal world. She surprised me by saying that not only does she want people to drop by, she actually has a few friends who do it. Afterward, I couldn't stop thinking about how to make dropping by work for me—creating opportunity for closer connection but inside boundaried spontaneity. Soon enough, I devised a plan and a few days after New Year's 2018, I sent this email to about twenty of my friends:

Hello, Friends,

Happy New Year! One of the things I struggle with as an extroverted only child is my desire to have loved ones casually in my home more often, but a discomfort with the idea that people would just unexpectedly drop by. So I want to create an opportunity for you all to drop by inside of a container of loose planning. In the coming year, I will send texts or emails up to a couple of days in advance to let you know you can come to Drop By Dinner. Here are guidelines:

1. These dinners will not be anything special and will be potluck-ish with a very low bar. I will feed you whatever I'm making for me and the kids. Bring something if you have it, even if it's just half a loaf of bread and a bit of cheese so we can make grilled cheese sandwiches.

2. This is CAYA[1] (come as you are). You do not have to be in a good mood, showered, party-ready, or up for socializing. I want us to have space to be our real, messy, human selves on these evenings. I might be in a crap mood or unshowered, and my house will most definitely be in some state of mess.

3. Campsite rules apply. Please make sure my home isn't messier when you leave than it was when you arrived. When I tell you to just leave the dishes in the sink, ignore me. Wash those shits.

4. Last-minute RSVPs and cancellations are fine. As are maybes. And last-minute cancellations on my part. Even if you don't RSVP, you can show up. THIS IS THE POINT!

5. You can bring your kids. Don't let a lack of childcare keep you from coming. My kids will be here.

6. You can't bring other adults. If you are getting this email, it's because I have a level of comfort with you that I want to deepen so we can be more real, vulnerable, and connected. I'm not trying to do that with all my friends or with your best friend who's visiting from out of town or with the lady you just met on Tinder. I don't even want to do it with your spouse.

Let me know if you have any questions or requests. And stay tuned for your first invitation sometime this month!

---

1. Shout-out to Yeshe Mathews for this acronym.

The email was met with enthusiasm and appreciation, and a couple of weeks later, I had my first Drop By Dinner. Some folks told me they were coming and came, others told me they were coming and didn't. Some folks didn't tell me they were coming and showed up anyway. Everyone brought food. I was wearing my pajamas. My sister-friends from Black Women's Freedom Circle had been in my home many times before. They helped themselves to my kitchen and exchanged familiar greetings with my kids. Others asked where things were—pot, colander, fork, bowl—but took charge of making food and feeding themselves and others once they had what they needed. There was sometimes awkwardness among the people who didn't know one another, but it seemed everyone gave each other the benefit of the doubt because they all knew each of them was important to me. Everyone ate; the dishes got washed. We crowded in the kitchen to talk and laugh. The evening ended with four of us sitting in the living room while Solomon brought us wine and popcorn and Stella put the food away and wiped down the counters (this is *not* normal behavior).

I've had several Drop By Dinners since the first one. Sometimes ten people show up, sometimes three. I truly love it. I feel like every time someone I love is in my house, they become less guest and more extended family.

THE ENTRY POINT FOR EVERYTHING

Saqib Keval has been living in the connections of food, family, community, and culture all his life. Like Jocelyn and Sita, for Saqib food was a thread, a language, and a medium before it was a vocation. Now, it's his "entry point for everything."

When I asked him what it is about food that is so conducive to bringing people together, he was very unromantic about it.

"The easy answer is, food is magical, and it's love, and people I love come to the table, and we're all together. But I think that's lazy, and I think that's white, and bullshit. Food isn't love. Food is struggle, and it's pain, and it's really difficult, and it's messy. And getting together is all of those things."

I think Saqib's clarity about the range of experiences and associations people can have with food is part of what makes his approach to food as a conduit to connection so thoughtful. He knows that kitchens and food can remind people of celebration and the safety of nourishing meals and relationships, but they can also bring up memories of violence, shaming about bodies and cooking, or obligatory labor. It's also that the people we end up at the literal or metaphorical table with may not always be people we like. People's Kitchen Collective is, among other things, an antidote to pain and an incubator for care.

People's Kitchen (before it was a collective) started in 2007 because Saqib was in college in Northern California and needed to build community and safety. He was in a conservative town with few people of color and the environment could be openly hostile: "I would go hiking and I would see burning crosses." Saqib got involved in political organizing efforts on campus and in the community and, in the process, got a political education. At the same time, he was working in restaurants. This meant that attending organizing meetings was hard because he worked in the evenings. So, for the first time, he brought food and social justice together. "I started hosting meals at the restaurant on off days. On Mondays, I'd usually come in to do prep work for the week, and I'd invite people to come in and have meetings there, so I could participate in them, and I would cook for them. Or we'd cook together."

With college and political education in hand, he went to France to continue university and train in French kitchens. He experienced a lot of racism and anti-immigration sentiment (white French people read him as a South Asian immigrant).

Saqib was working with a great chef in a demanding restaurant. They worked closely together, going to the markets early every morning to pick up orders before going to the restaurant to start the day's prep work. They saw the same farmers and vendors every day, but if Saqib had to go back without the chef later in the day to pick up an order that hadn't come in earlier, they would refuse to deal with him. "I wouldn't get let into bars and restaurants; I wouldn't get served; I would not be allowed to enter certain spaces because a doorman would tell me, 'Oh, there's a quota for dark-skinned men.' It wasn't one place, it was many places. It was more normal than it was not."

Saqib connected with North African, Moroccan, and other Black and brown men working in kitchens around town. Since they couldn't eat out, they would get together and cook for themselves, talking and sharing with one another.

When Saqib returned to the States, he moved into a collective house with radical people of color who, as part of living together, committed to creating projects in their community. People's Kitchen began to solidify as a project for Saqib as he organized antigentrification meals in San Francisco's Mission District. "It was a very Filipino, Korean, Salvadoran,

Black, and Mexican neighborhood, all mixed together. And everyone was getting pushed out. The meals presented the history of families that had been living there and brought together a mix of people from the neighborhood to have conversations about resisting gentrification. Organizing conversations would all happen around the guise of having a really nice meal: you're welcome to come cook with us, and while we eat, these are some of the conversations that'll happen at the table." These meals lifted up history and cultures that were being pushed out and erased from the community—the very same cultures that attracted gentrifiers in the first place.

Gentrification ultimately pushed them out as well, and Saqib took People's Kitchen across the bay to Oakland. He was working at People's Grocery, a food security organization in West Oakland (which is where we met). He would occasionally go into Cosecha, a home-style Mexican spot in Oakland's historic Swan's Market, to eat and hang out. He got to know chef and owner Dominica Rice-Cisneros and her partner, Carlos Salomon. He talked with them about his evolving idea for People's Kitchen. They would hold events built on the antigentrification meals model that People's Kitchen had started in the Mission, adding performances, music, art, and storytelling. Dominica and Carlos offered to help. "They just gave me their space. They were like, 'This is an amazing project, a really good idea, whatever we can do to support.' Every month they gave us their restaurant and they didn't charge anything. I used their pots and pans. When we ran out of olive oil, Dominica would pull out her really expensive olive oil that she uses at her restaurant, she's passing me gallons of it. 'Use this, use this. Let me pull you some wine!'"

People's Kitchen held monthly meals at Cosecha. Tables and chairs, borrowed from a church, were dropped off via the church bus on Saturday afternoon and picked up late Saturday night to be used for Sunday service. A "volunteer kitchen crew, and volunteer servers, and a bunch of elders and aunties" would cook out of Cosecha and the church, creating meals that served up to two hundred people. Each meal benefited a different partner organization, raising up to $3,500 for them. These were not nonprofit organizations; these were small grassroots projects that didn't have the funds or infrastructure to raise foundation money.

Food was the point of entry for People's Kitchen to do their work. "The organizing approach to People's Kitchen is, you can politicize someone much more easily if their mouth is full. So, you can talk and can engage with them, and you just keep shoving food down their mouth. They'll be happy, you'll be happy, and at the end you spent two hours breaking down a complex thought or something. And when they have a sweet part of dessert, people can ask questions, and everyone's calm now, and over any discomfort or anger, because they just had a meal."

Saqib also wants people to have the experience of being cared for, a skill he fine-tuned in high-end restaurants, which, unsurprisingly, he has a love-hate relationship with.

"A lot of them have honed a very particular type of hospitality to an art. They've learned how to study body language and anticipate people's needs. To be a good server, you know what your guests need before they know that they need it. Before you even sniffle, someone is showing up with a tissue, because they heard your voice, and they've seen your red eyes, and they have seen what's going on with you as you're coming to the restaurant, as you're sitting down, as you're at the table. And they know that you're probably going to need a tissue. So, they'll be there ready with a tissue. And before you're done with the tissue, they're there with a container to take it away."

That care is cultivated at his own restaurant, Masala y Maiz, which he and his wife, Norma Listman, opened in Mexico City in 2017. "It's based on something that's very familial for me. When it's done really well, it should feel like you're being cared for by a member of your family. Not someone you're paying for the service of being cared for, but someone who has a legitimate, vested interest in your well-being and your care and your comfort, and that's not monetary. Of course, it is. But the magic is that it shouldn't feel like that."

I experienced that art of care at that first PKC meal that I attended at Life Is Living in 2013. When we got there, I felt excited and a little overwhelmed by the crowd and the scene. I didn't know anyone. There's a kind of isolation I sometimes felt as a mother out in the world with my children when they were younger. As wonderful as my babies were, they are demanding and wanted to explore, be held, be fed, have my attention. And public mothering, particularly as a Black woman, so often had me feeling both invisible and conspicuous. When we were approached at our table by a PKC volunteer, there was a quality to the interaction that immediately made me feel seen and welcome. I no longer felt apart from the crowd. It remains one of my most powerful experiences of belonging in an environment where I didn't know anyone. It taught me something about what it looks like to see strangers and welcome them.

Accessibility is another dimension of this craft as well. Saqib explains, "It should be accessible in every sense, the location, the price, the feel, the number of steps leading up to it, everything about it should be thought through. Because again, it needs to be accessible because you're anticipating people's needs, and you're valuing their presence, and you're thinking about all the ways that they can be present, and you're trying to remove all the barriers."

Saqib honed his approach in college, France, and the Bay Area, but it all started at home with his family. "My family are immigrants from North India that have been in East Africa for over two hundred and fifty years. And then from there they migrated all over the world, nearly all the continents. I can't escape them; they're everywhere."

Saqib's family in the States has a long-standing tradition of coming together to prepare and eat meals that can include one hundred to two hundred family members. When he told me this, I was a bit incredulous. The idea that a family, as opposed to an organization or cultural center, would hold monthly meals that size seemed incredible to me. But, now I know. And the key is spreadsheets.

"There's spreadsheets that have lists of who is here, who's in the meal, when you're cooking, and when you're responsible for cleaning, and everything. So, you know what date the gathering's happening, where it's happening, and what you're responsible for bringing." Households rotate setup, cooking, and cleaning duties, and the location rotates houses, with most meals happening around Sacramento, and people driving in from as far away as Los Angeles.

Whoever is hosting moves all their furniture to the garage or outside and fills the floors with sheets, blankets, and pillows so everyone can sit and eat on the floor, though there are tables for the elders. There are storage units at various houses with all the equipment necessary to pull off these meals. "At one house, they have the storage unit with all the chairs. Another house has a storage unit with all the plastic folding tables. Someone else has all the stoves and cookware. And things just basically move from house to house as needed."

Knowing all of this made me understand how Saqib envisioned a volunteer crew of people creating meals that could serve hundreds—this is what he grew up in.

THIS IS HOW THE COLLECTIVE MADE IT

In 2018, Stella and I volunteered for two days to cook and serve at a PKC event called To the STREETS. This event was the culmination of a yearlong series called "From the FARM, to the KITCHEN, to the TABLE, to the STREETS." Every event included delicious, meaning-filled food, readings, performance, and political education.

Bringing together farmers, artists, chefs, and activists, From the FARM asked attendees to think about how they are, or have historically been, connected to land and the cultivation of food. "The farm exists both as a place of liberation and trauma, simultaneously. The farm has been a plantation. It is also where we have grown and sown the seeds of our homes," Jocelyn explained.

To the Kitchen: A People's Remedies Stand was a recognition that "The remedies are in our kitchens." Attendees got to read and share "kitchen remedies" that PKC had collected from hundreds of people around the world—the kinds of things our parents, elders, or caretakers gave us when were sick. It included remedies for everything from sore throats and earaches to anxiety and heartbreak to white supremacy and homophobia.

To the TABLE focused on solidarity work among Arab, Asian, Black, and Latinx Americans and immigrants in remembrance of the signing of Executive Order 9066, in which President Franklin D. Roosevelt authorized the internment of 112,000 people of Japanese descent. We ate incredible Japanese food and learned about the impact of internment on Japanese families in the Bay Area, and their resistance to it. At this meal, I learned the practice of everyone at a table taking collective responsibility for making sure that all of us are served. (Saqib told me, "We serve food family style because it's not about you, the individual. You eating is contingent on everyone else eating.")

To the STREETS was a free, seated community meal for five hundred people. There was a volunteer meeting where I began to understand all the intention and thought that took place behind PKC events. The design of that meeting was meant to bring everyone there into closer connection with one another. We were asked what people of color–centered hospitality looks like to us, and got into small groups to discuss. When we reported back to the larger group, we said things like, "There's never a thing of there's not enough food; you just stretch it, just make it work. And you make people feel welcome"; "There aren't hosts and guests, there's shared labor. So, if you're a guest, that doesn't mean you don't go into the kitchen and help out, it doesn't mean you don't wash the dishes"; and "Respect, even if you have a relative that you kind of don't like what she makes, but then you still respect her, you still accept it with gratitude."

They helped us all understand that everyone was welcome, but that welcoming people is active, not passive. And that our orientation toward the people who would be eating the meal was, "We do not serve you, we are being of service to you, as you are being of service to the person sitting next to you."

Two weeks later was the event. The request for help is one of the beautiful things PKC practices. It is not begging for volunteers, it is an invitation to be part of something bigger than yourself, to cocreate. "Cooking with us is not about production," Saqib told me, "but it's about the experience. Which is a vastly different experience than working in any restaurant, right? Things happen slowly, so we intentionally plan for them to happen slowly. And things get messed up and redone, and reworked or whatever. Or not. And we're just like, okay, this is how the collective has made this dish, so this is what we're serving. And it might be very different from what we thought. But, you know, it's what's happening."

Stella and I spent a Saturday afternoon doing a kitchen shift—making cornbread and compound butter, slicing vegetables, and shredding chicken. When we first walked into the industrial kitchen PKC has secured to cook the meal, there were at least twenty people at work. We were greeted by several of them and shown where to wash our hands and get snacks during breaks. Saqib explained, "All the things that I think about in service and hosting and restaurant work, Sita thinks about that in terms of who are the people working with us: How do you make them feel good, and make sure that the snacks are always available, and plentiful so it feels abundant?"

There was a lot of work to do, but incredible organization and planning combined with "enough bodies in the space doing work so that people can take rests whenever they want and don't feel pressured to produce" meant that it was easy to step into a role and feel part of a supportive, powerful experience. Stella and I both felt a clear sense of purpose, a sense of being valued that encouraged our own generosity.

The To the TABLE event lifted up the story of connection between Japanese internment and racist anti-immigrant and anti-Muslim sentiment in America today. The Reverend Marvin K. White, a poet and public theologian, recited a poem he'd written for the occasion. In it, he said, "Everything is a gathering and a calling home. I want people to know they are welcomed and, more importantly, expected." He does not say he wants people to *feel* expected, but to know they *are* expected. I love this openhearted stance alongside the call to show up. A meal can be an opportunity to soften our edges and open ourselves to learning and loving one another. It can be a way through grief and conflict toward solace and understanding. But Saqib is right that food, and the gathering that goes along with it, can be messy and hard and traumatic. No amount of dessert makes someone's devil's advocacy or disregard okay.

Saqib, Jocelyn, and Sita show me that we can truly welcome people to our literal and metaphoric tables while also insisting they have good table manners. Good manners is not about being polite. It's about gratitude and recognition of all that led to us being at the table. It's about sharing in the labor of making the table a place for all of us to be seen and accepted. And when we transgress—when we offend, neglect, or fail to show up well—we must clean up our mess by being accountable and working to do better next time. We can expect people's presence and also expect *of* them behavior that contributes to everyone's sense of welcome and belonging.

EIGHT

We Can't Build Safety Without Community

Healing, Repair, and Accountability

> We are each other's harvest; we are each other's
> business; we are each other's magnitude and bond.
> —GWENDOLYN BROOKS

I N 1998, I attended the first Critical Resistance conference and learned about the prison industrial complex and the modern abolition movement. It's also where I first started questioning my fundamental understanding of safety.

"Real security is *not* locking up more and more people," scholar and activist Ruthie Wilson Gilmore told us. "Real security is knowing that you will have shelter, that you will have food, that you will have beauty in your life. That you have a future, that your family has a future."

That conference was for me the beginning of ten years of volunteering and organizing for Critical Resistance and my abiding, though imperfect, stance as an abolitionist.

The modern abolition movement challenges us to interrogate our beliefs about what safety is, how it is achieved or preserved, and what it costs us and others. It challenges us to recognize that prisons, policing, surveillance, and other structures that make up the prison industrial complex (PIC) are ineffective solutions to social problems. It asks us to understand that the PIC causes tremendous harm, not just to people cast as "criminals" or "wrongdoers," but to families and communities, and ultimately all of us. Further, abolition is not just about the absence of policing and prisons. It's about the presence of systems and cultures of support that actually create well-being. We know what those things are— physical and mental health care, housing, well-paying jobs, well-funded schools, time to spend with loves ones and do things that bring us joy and purpose, maybe even things like a guaranteed income.[1]

The future I was invited to imagine back in 1998 felt both exhilarating and terrifying. Not terrifying because of the absence of police and prisons, but because dreaming that big was uncomfortable. But with the leadership and patient support of amazing thinkers and humans, like Ruthie, Rachel Herzing, and Rose Braz (rest in peace and power), among many others, I was encouraged to realign my beliefs with my values, head, and heart, and imagine the world of my wildest, most hopeful dreams.

Ruthie's words that day in 1998 introduced me to something I didn't know I was looking for—another version of life that says my safety is grounded in positive things like care and love, and that I have a responsibility to not abandon others to struggle on their own. It said that all of us are deserving

---

1. Guaranteed income, also known as basic income, is a policy idea that would unconditionally provide a periodic payment from the government to everyone in a city, state, or country. It would be enough money to meet a person's basic needs.

of the things we need to live. We don't have to earn it, and we can't unearn it. This is in such stark contrast to American Dreamism—the toxic individualism, the winners and losers, the demand that we prove our worth by being "productive members of society." I want, as Ruthie wrote with journalist and former prisoner James Kilgore, "a society that centers freedom and justice instead of profit and punishment."[2] And part of what I've come to realize is that it's not unrealistic or utopian, because it's happening.

There are people practicing the philosophy of abolition in their daily lives, making real what they imagine, and creating practices based on an understanding of safety grounded in mutuality and care that says none of us is disposable, all of us should get what we need to live, and that the only way you do that is in connected community.

WE DREAMED UP HOMEFULLNESS

The house sits on a long lot. There is new construction in the front—the windows still have retail stickers on them and the exterior walls are covered with house wrap. I pass a trailer, which I later learn houses a radio station, and then see a yard that has a couple of goats in it. There, to the right, is a structure that looks like it could be occupied. When I enter the house, there is a group of five or six Black and brown middle school–aged boys sitting on couches, notebooks in hand, listening intently to their teacher, a Black man with a trim

---

2. Ruth Wilson Gilmore and James Kilgore, "The Case for Abolition," The Marshall Project, June 6, 2019, https://www.themarshallproject.org/2019/06/19/the-case-for-abolition.

beard, wearing a hoodie. In front of me is a kitchen and the young woman with long, dark hair at the sink looks up at me when I walk in. I let her know I'm there to see Tiny.

Tiny's room is just off the living room. We sit on the bed to talk and are occasionally quietly interrupted by one of the boys as they go through her room to get to the bathroom. We always stop talking so she can introduce them to me. Each boy looks me in the eye and shakes my hand. They are confident, but not with the aggressiveness that men and boys are sometimes taught to greet people—the power play. These boys are gentle and grounded.

They attend the Decolonization Academy, a school for "houseless and formerly houseless children" that takes place at Homefullness. Homefullness is a "sweat equity, permanent co-housing, education, arts, micro-business and social change project for landless/houseless and formerly houseless families and individuals." The folks at Homefullness are creating their own solutions to homelessness.

I first became aware of Tiny around 2006, when I heard a segment on a local radio station. It was from the folks at POOR Magazine, a journalism project by and for poor people. I don't remember exactly what Tiny was talking about, but I remember feeling both curious and inspired. Since then, I've kept up with some of the work they've done—like when they started a summer program and the school. I also read Tiny's memoir, *Criminal of Poverty: Growing Up Homeless in America*, which is a beautiful piece of storytelling.[3] Tiny has a million stories. Her stories can be hilarious, heartbreaking,

---

3. Lisa Gray-Garcia, *Criminal of Poverty: Growing Up Homeless in America* (San Francisco: City Lights Foundation Books, 2006).

poignant, devastating, and joyful. When she tells them, she feels all the emotion she is evoking—she cracks up, she cries, she gets pissed, she grins. She writes and speaks with words that reframe the meaning of language we use all the time. "American dream" becomes "AmeriKlan scheme," "landlord" becomes "scamlord," "capitalist system" becomes "crapitalist system." I admit that when I first encountered this language swapping, I internally rolled my eyes at it. It seemed overzealous. But now I appreciate how it continually pulls me into a slightly heightened and sometimes uncomfortable awareness of how political our everyday language is.

Tiny grew up in California with her mom, Dee. Dee was an orphan and they had no family support. When Tiny was eleven, the funding for Dee's job as a social worker ran out. Dee's descent into depression, her chronic health issues, and recurrences of PTSD (born of the abuse, neglect, and torture she experienced as a foster child) made getting another job impossible and they became homeless. Tiny dropped out of school to care for her mother and hustle money. They made and sold art, navigated and hacked systems to get what they needed to live. For example, Dee was brown-skinned (Irish and Afro–Puerto Rican), but Tiny is white-passing and has light hair and blue eyes. So, when Tiny was twelve, her mom bought her a suit and Tiny would convince landlords that she was in her twenties and had a solid salary. With no documentation (this was the '80s), she would sign a lease and they would have an apartment until their money ran out and they got evicted.

While they were scraping and surviving, Dee and Tiny were also dreaming. "We were living in our car, on bus benches when the cars were stolen, parks, sleeping in doorways, anything and everywhere. And together—because we would have this beautiful symbiotic way—she would dream and I would manifest; that was kind of our thing. We were having these conversations and doing art about our life while we were living it, and that's when we dreamed up Homefullness."

They started building toward it with Mamahouses, collective homes run by mothers for single parents and their children. The first one came out of writing workshops Dee and Tiny were doing. Tiny had taught herself how to write grants. In 1997, they got some funding to do these workshops with poor mothers. "I get this grant; Mom's like, 'Okay, well that's ten Gs to do writing workshops and pay stipends for unhoused families and mamas. So that means that we need to make sure that those mamas are housed, right?' And she's like, 'Take these four Gs and go get a frickin' house for the women and children that we're going to do these workshops for.' And we did. That was the first Mamahouse."

Tiny and her mother worked with a group of women in that house to write what became volume 2 of *POOR Magazine*, which focused on health care. They worked together, ate together, spent time together—remaking the village, as Tiny explained to me. They were much more than housemates. They were lifesaving connection and belonging for each other. "Isolation kills," she told me. "And for single-parent women, that's a different kind of beast, it really is. It really almost killed us many times."

The first Mamahouse ended when they ran out of money to pay the rent. The foundation that granted them money wasn't interested in funding housing for poor people because they funded only art programs for poor people. It was a level of hypocrisy that is, as Tiny so pointedly puts it, "hypocrazy."

The loss of this home was devastating because without a central location, the families had to go wherever they could find housing or support—some ending up back on the street—and they couldn't find those things together. But Dee and Tiny knew that the failure to keep the house going was not on them, but on the systems and structures that make it nearly impossible for their community members to get by.

There were two more iterations of the Mamahouses. The second Mamahouse was an apartment in a building overrun with pigeons, rats, and roaches. Right after one of the mamas complained to the rent board about the conditions of the building, their apartment suspiciously caught fire and the Mamahouse residents were once more scattered.

The last Mamahouse was a dream. It was a beautiful, light-filled house with spacious rooms, a big kitchen, and a yard with fruit trees. Tiny and her friend Laure pooled their skills and resources to secure the house. In that home, they housed multiple families, sharing food, care, resources, and support. They made art, rehearsed plays, and held workshops. In that home, they created their Declaration of Interdependence and the Manifesto of Change, handwritten documents that anchor and articulate Homefullness's approach and values.

When they lost the last house, Tiny's son sat outside on a box full of Legos and said, "Mama, it's ok, I just figured it out, we are going to move to Homefullness after this, and then we will all be ok."[4] While they moved in and out of several temporary living situations, the next place they came together with community again to live was Homefullness.

---

4. Lisa "Tiny" Gray-Garcia, "Capitalism Killed Mamahouse," *POOR Magazine*, October 7, 2010, https://www.poormagazine.org/node/3333.

Tiny and the POOR Magazine community push me to rethink so much of how I've come to understand my political analysis. For example, "culture of poverty," as I've understood it, is the victim-blaming notion that poor people have "bad" values and morals and weak work ethics and are to blame for perpetuating generational poverty. But when Tiny says "culture of poverty," it's not a condemnation. It's about the shared experience of knowing what it's like to miss a meal, of having to navigate systems that assume the worst of you, of carrying the trauma of living on the street, experiencing state and interpersonal violence, of being criminalized. It's a shared experience that creates a bond that can bridge over differences in geography and race. "There's this sort of cross-cultural, cross-racial, cross-linguistic connection between 'poverty skolas,'" she explained.

Homefullness and the POOR Magazine community are people who make it up as they go along with the brilliance and creativity of people who have always had to forge their own path forward. They have a media company that publishes magazines and books, they have a radio station, a café, a school, a training institute, and arts organization. They have the scrappiness and determination of people who've been told "you can't" their whole lives but realized that if the paths toward "success" aren't for them, then neither are the rules of failure.

Tiny pushes back against any inclination to romanticize Homefullness. "These folks coming together is extremely powerful," Tiny told me. "And also we come with all our trauma. And it's extreme. And now we're trauma hitting trauma, which is really, really deep. All of that lead to this beautiful manifestation of a co-living situation rooted in our collective need, as poor parents and children. The themes were need-based at their core. It wasn't because of a utopic vision that it would be good to have community."

There were very practical needs the residents of Mama-houses provided for each other. Childcare was a big piece of it, but this was not childcare just to enable working or going to school. It was about getting time to deal with stress or take a break. "If I did not get out in the morning and get just thirty minutes away from that baby, I really was going to lose it, on the real," Tiny told me.

They also shared resources. "You got some EBT cash, I don't. Let's share that, because we're going to eat tomorrow, we're going to eat together. Rent money. I didn't get my welfare check, or I blew it, or I didn't have it, or I had to pay it for a bill that fucking was way more than the three hundred and forty-one dollars. Okay, I'll use some of my SSI check, we'll get this paid, and we won't be out of here."

In the decades that the POOR Magazine community have been at it, they have accumulated tremendous wisdom and knowledge about how to do what they do. They have set up councils of community members to deal with decision-making, conflict, and harm. They run workshops to educate people with wealth about who and where their money came from, and how to redistribute it. They've developed processes to heal from trauma and mental illness, including creating a network of Revolutionary Love Workers—therapists, somatic healers, and social workers who provide free or low-cost care. They decolonize education, food, relationships with government systems, relationships with people who have wealth, and their relationships with one another. They wrote a book, *Poverty Scholarship: Poor People-Led Theory, Art, Words and*

Tears Across Mama Earth, which makes much of their wisdom and practice available.[5] Because that's the thing we need, of course, more examples that allow us to see that something else is not just possible, but being lived by people every day.

I love, and am shook by, all Homefullness calls into question for me about how I'm in relationship with people, how I parent, what I expect from others and from the institutions I interact with. Being at Homefullness made me feel a familiar longing for a deeper, closer village—a sense that me and some group of people are all in for one another. But it also revealed the beautiful possibility of something deep and right: the intention toward community and land, the wisdom gathered—remembered, really—over decades, and the commitment to a set of shared values.

MAKING JUSTICE TOGETHER

In my own neighborhood, Oakland Communities United for Equity and Justice (OCUEJ) has been working in a quickly gentrifying community at the points where conflict and disconnect occur. When violence happens in the neighborhood, OCUEJ reaches out to the victims and/or their family to see what they need. The support it offers is things like holding barbecues and planting memorial trees in a neighborhood park. But what that does is address the invisibility we often experience after a loved one dies or we experience trauma. In a neighborhood with the diminishing ties brought by

5. Lisa "Tiny" Gray-Garcia, Dee Garcia, and POOR Magazine, *Poverty Scholarship: Poor People-Led Theory, Art, Words and Tears Across Mama Earth* (Oakland, CA: Poor Press, 2019).

gentrification, the people who live around you may have no idea that you're suffering. OCUEJ helps families make their loss more shared and less isolating.

OCUEJ also holds drives to get requested supplics for the encampments of unhoused people closest to us and runs several community and school-based gardens, a community-supported agriculture (CSA) subscription service, youth entrepreneurial programs, and restorative justice training.

The collective folds many of these actions into one another. Take the Driver Plaza Community Memorial Orchard. Driver Plaza was a neglected strip of park awkwardly located in a triangle created by three streets intersecting. It was the sight of both gun violence and the "violence of gentrification." Auntie Frances, a longtime community member who for years has coordinated a weekly meal in the park through her Self-Help Hunger Program, called for change in the park and insisted upon "public land for public good." "With our partners we decided to bring new and old community members together and plant a fruit tree every time there was grief, loss, struggle, or tragedy."[6] As a result, Phat Beets, which is part of OCUEJ, planted over sixty fruit trees.

OCUEJ also intervenes in moments when neighbors might call the police. Max Kurtz-Kadji, an OCUEJ cofounder, tracks conversations on the neighborhood Facebook and Nextdoor pages. A conversation started about a man in a trench coat. "There was this guy wandering around and some folks thought he was casing cars and they wanted to call the police. This was over two days; no one saw him break in the car. We were like, 'Well, then, why are you calling the police?'

6. Phat Beets Produce, http://phatbeetsproduce.org/urban-gardens.

'Because he's acting funny.' Well, isn't it his right to walk around in a trench coat?" Max reached out to the police captain, with whom he has forged a relationship, to say that police intervention was not called for and asked for some resources that might be helpful to the man. The police captain did some research and gave Max mental health services information. Additionally, Max went out to try to talk to the man and see what he needed. Although that conversation didn't get far, neighbors got to see another way of addressing human beings who make them uncomfortable. Another OCUEJ member, Mustafa, shares his number with neighbors so if there are "strange men" or loud kids or people yelling or playing music too late, there's someone to call besides the police.

OCUEJ's approach brings abolition to life. As Critical Resistance cofounder Rachel Herzing once explained to me, one of the ways we reduce policing is by just not calling the police. If we don't rely on them, it becomes harder to justify investing in them. We can tell people, particularly white people, to stop calling the cops on Black people for barbecuing, sitting in Starbucks without ordering, napping in their dormitory common room, swimming in their community pool, cleaning up their own yards, using coupons . . . the list is truly endless. And some will begin to understand that they are risking a Black person's well-being, and potentially their life, when they call the cops on them. But when conflict actually happens, we need some better options than doing nothing or calling the police. What OCUEJ is trying to do is build another system, one that shortens the distance between people who live in the same neighborhood and prioritizes genuine safety.

But harm happens, and it most often happens among people in relationships—partners, family members, coworkers, neighbors, peers. To truly support the healing of people who experience harm, and to have justice and accountability, we need a process that recognizes the real complexities of com munities and relationships and addresses the conditions—specific and systemic—that promote harm.

This is where transformative justice (TJ) comes in. Mia Mingus, a TJ practitioner and disability justice advocate, describes transformative justice simply as a "way of responding to violence and harm that doesn't create more violence and harm. People have called it a way of getting in right relationship with each other, or a way of making justice together."

She goes on to explain, "So, we're not relying on the police, prisons, the criminal legal system, the courts, et cetera. And then, I think most importantly, it helps to cultivate the very things that we know prevent future violence, harm, and abuse. Things like safety, resilience, accountability, healing, et cetera for everybody involved."

As Ejeris Dixon, a renowned transformative justice educator and practitioner, explained to me, TJ is an approach that "recognizes that interpersonal harm is rooted in oppression and works to change conditions that create, maintain, sustain, and support oppression, exploitation, domination and harm. . . . [It] works to meet individual needs for justice (safety, healing, repair, connection, accountability) while also working towards a long-term vision for liberation."

Although TJ emerged from fields addressing childhood sexual abuse, domestic violence, and sexual assault, its application extends far beyond those forms of harm.

Dr. Mimi Kim, a professor at California State University, Long Beach, is a longtime anti–domestic violence advocate and an expert in transformative justice approaches to violence intervention and prevention. She grew up in Minnesota with parents who immigrated to the States from Korea. Her mother was from South Korea; her father, North Korea. The national divisions her parents experienced influenced the psychic backdrop of her work in domestic violence and sexual assault. "Everything dealing with the harm and the conflict of violence was to separate people, and yet I've come from a family that was really violated by that separation itself."

Mimi started doing work to address sexual assault in the late '80s, and shortly after that started working in the field of domestic violence in Asian communities. What she found in those fields was an approach that was based on rigid narratives about perpetrators and victims. "Everything was about dealing with the harm; the [approach toward] sexual and domestic violence then was to separate people." But Mimi saw that families in her community were being harmed by the separations. She found herself implementing approaches that she wouldn't use herself or that she knew her family wouldn't have accepted.

Mimi had seen her mother do it a different way. "My mother was called upon to help people who were in a domestic violence situation; people came to her. They were looking for an answer." What Mimi realized is that people go to those they trust and respect for support and advice. And when it came to the intimacy of sexual assault and domestic violence, those trusted folks are first responders.

In order to both build on and capture how people rely on their own social ties to get support and intervene when they experience interpersonal violence, Mimi developed Creative Interventions.[7] In addition to capturing dozens of stories, the organization created the exhaustive six-hundred-plus-page "Creative Interventions Toolkit: A Practical Guide to Stop Interpersonal Violence" with the goal of promoting:

> [A]n approach called community-based interventions to violence or what some call community accountability or transformative justice as a way to break isolation and to create solutions to violence from those who are most affected by violence—survivors and victims of violence, friends, family and community. It asks us to look to those around us to gather together to create grounded, thoughtful community responses. It builds on our connections and caring rather than looking at solutions that rely only on separation and disconnections from our communities. It invites us to involve even those who harm us as potential allies in stopping that harm and as active partners in deeply changing attitudes and behaviors towards a solution to violence. It expands the idea of violence and its solutions from that between individuals to one that includes communities—both close and intimate communities and the broader communities of which we are a part.

Healing, repair, and accountability is something every survivor should be able to expect. But our systems are not set up to deliver these things. Further, people experience violence, violation, and harassment from systems that are ostensibly set

---

7. Creative Interventions is "a resource center to create and promote *community-based responses to interpersonal violence*." Learn more at http://www.creative-interventions.org/about/.

up to keep them safe—police, courts, child protective services, the foster care system, medical professionals and hospitals.

Truly preventing harm means that we have to support the transformation of those who perpetrate it. This creates a very real tension. For example, when it comes to sexual harassment and assault, the United States is finally just beginning to actually pay attention to and believe survivors. But still, there is a deeply entrenched practice of making excuses for perpetrators, and blaming survivors. A focus on accountability from, and transformation of, perpetrators can't happen at the expense of victims and survivors. It can't be an excuse to continue to ignore, dismiss, and gaslight survivors. But it *is* necessary. If we are serious about actually reducing future violence, locking up, banishing, and throwing out perpetrators isn't going to get us there.

Mimi made clear to me that transformative justice takes time and stamina. Unlike the criminal legal system, which offers neither healing or accountability, transformative justice requires that everyone involved—the victim, the perpetrator, people who choose to be support people to either of them, people who witnessed the harm, and the facilitators—own the process of not only seeking justice, but defining what it looks like. Instead of abdicating the process to courts and lawyers, the community must do the work.

Mia Mingus told me that the process is challenging for all the reasons you'd expect—it's painful and uncomfortable, and people come to the process with varying understandings of the approach—but it's also logistically difficult because there are a lot of people involved.

There are many ways to facilitate a TJ process, and Mia made clear to me that the process she uses is what works for her and the people she works with. Other facilitators have different processes. But here's the gist:

The process only happens if the people involved fully consent to it. Both the harmer and the survivor have a team of support people they meet with regularly, and representatives from each group must also meet regularly to keep the process focused and moving. The survivor's team is made up of people they trust who can help them in their healing. For the harmer, it's people they trust and who can support them in holding themselves accountable for what they did.

With the help of their team, the survivor creates a survivor statement. This articulates what happened and what they want from the transformative justice process. These statements can include requests they have from the harmer. Mia gave me several examples: a closing circle with the harmer, disclosing the harm they caused and the TJ process to anyone they date for the next three years, going to therapy, moving out of their shared neighborhood, stepping back from leadership, and paying for the survivor's therapy. The survivor's support team uses the statement to frame the survivor's healing. The accountability team uses it as their blueprint to work with the perpetrator toward accountability for what happened.

Of course, it's not straightforward. Even just pulling support teams together can be a challenge. Many of us have people who we can talk to when we're harmed. But how many of us have people we'd feel comfortable talking with about a horrible thing we've done, who would also be effective at supporting us in our accountability? Reflecting some of the bad behavior we've seen through the media, Mia explained that "people end up colluding with abusers or reinforcing the shaming and blaming of survivors in their attempt to support someone in taking accountability for harm." Additionally, people who˙cause harm, especially if it's violence, are often abandoned by their community. "What I tell people all the time is if you're not actively cultivating relationships in your life where you can have conversations about accountability, then you are actively cultivating an unaccountable life. You have to be putting in the time and energy for yourself. It's basically like a fire drill or an earthquake drill. And most of us have done a fire drill, an earthquake drill, and that happens way less than sexual assault."

I'm going to share a story with you that Mia shared with me because it helped me understand what goes into the transformative justice process. But it's a story about sexual assault, so it's upsetting and may be hard to read. There are no descriptions of the assault. But if you *do not* want to read about a sexual assault perpetrator and survivor's process, skip ahead to the text after the horizontal line on page 206. And to be clear, like many of the other names and details in this book, the names and details in this story have been changed.

Javier and Damon were part of an activist group. Damon, who is an undocumented immigrant, was one of the leaders of the group and held a lot of positional power and status in the group. He raped Javier. Javier, who is documented, did not want to involve the police. Mia explained to me that this is not uncommon: "Many, many survivors call me because they don't want to go to the system, because it's not just harmers that get harmed by the system. Survivors are too." This is even more likely when the community is made up of gay, trans, and gender-nonconforming people with varied immigrations status. I think it's important to underscore how regular it is that people who are marginalized—queer folks, sex workers, unhoused people, poor people, Black, brown, and Indigenous folks—are regularly disrespected, victimized, and hurt by the police when they call them for help.

The members of the activist group attempted several processes to find some kind of resolution. Not only did it not work, but the community fractured—people took sides. So, Mia was called in. The process took more than a year, and included not only working with the harmer and the survivor but with their community—anyone who was impacted by the harm. This included trainings on transformative justice philosophy and practice. Mia does this because the harm she's helping to address may not be the only harm happening in the community, and also because the next time harm happens—which it will—she wants people to be more prepared to respond.

When Mia enters the scene, there's often an absence of the kind of relationship cohesion that can provide the support necessary for the harmer and the survivor, and not much understanding of transformative justice as a framework. This was the case with Javier, Damon, and their community, so a lot of her work early on was making sure Javier was being supported and educating everyone about TJ.

In this instance, one of the things Javier articulated in his survivor's statement was the desire for a closing circle with Damon. This is not uncommon, though,

Mia explained, it's critical that the survivor's healing not be tied to any particular outcome or response from the harmer. But it meant that Damon would have to admit what he'd done and be clear about how he would change his behavior.

Mia described to me the process she took Damon through—from him admitting that what he'd done was unwanted sexual contact to being able to say to Javier, during the closing circle, "I'm sorry I raped you." Hearing it made me uncomfortable. Later, I sat with that discomfort and realized part of it was imagining a survivor and the person who assaulted them in a room together talking about the assault. But my discomfort came from other things too. Like, how unheard of it is for people who experience violence to get real accountability from those who hurt them. And how rare it is that a perpetrator's behavior is addressed so they are less likely to harm others. We have such a low bar when it comes to our expectations for resolving harm and tending to healing and accountability, and we are all suffering for it.

Given how hard this work is and how little support she and others get for it, I wanted to know why Mia does it. She told me, "Any time a survivor comes to me and wants a TJ process, it gives me hope. Especially when anyone who heard their story would easily say they would be justified in punishment or revenge. Any time someone who has done harm decides to be part of a TJ process and face what they've done or seeks support for their own accountability, that gives me hope. I am constantly inspired by ordinary people's courage and vulnerability; by the power of truth, love, faith, and the work of building back our shared humanity. As a survivor, nothing has been more healing or transformative for me than doing this work."

American Dreamism suggests that healing from trauma is a solitary process that survivors have to take charge of and move forward on their own. It also says an individual is solely responsible for the harm they cause and, as such, should be blamed and punished. As for the rest of us, we should mind our own business—until we become the harmer or the survivor. So, we keep being right and righteous instead of doing the hard work of being in deep community with people and showing up for all the healing that's necessary.

What Mia said about cultivating an accountable life made me think hard about my relationships. I've talked with some of my people about supporting my accountability when it comes to my values and the integrity of my politics, but I'd never thought about it in terms of my harmful behavior toward people in my community. I have a hard time imagining a situation in which I'd need to be held accountable for sexual assault or other kinds of violence. But, of course, people who perpetrate those harms likely think the same thing. Regardless, I definitely hurt people sometimes. So do you. Explicitly talking with people we're close to about helping us be accountable for harm we cause is yet another opportunity to bring people in a bit closer, expose more of our vulnerability, and build intimacy.

Because most of us haven't thought too deeply about that, the Bay Area Transformative Justice Collective, of which Mia is a founding member, created a process called "pod mapping." A pod is "the people that you would call on if violence, harm or abuse happened to you; or the people that you would call on if you wanted support in taking accountability for violence, harm or abuse that you've done; or if you witnessed violence or if someone you care about was being violent or being abused."[8] You might have multiple pods, depending on what kind of support is required.

We are responsible for one another. That doesn't mean we can heal someone or make them accountable, though—they have to own a commitment to those things. But it does mean being there. It means not avoiding our people when they experience trauma, illness, violence, or pain we find hard or scary. It means not abandoning people to their relentless pain and hurting. It also means collecting our folks when they mess up. "If you're proactively building an accountable life," Mia told me, "you need to realize that everybody you're in relationship with—if they do some shit, then you are the person who has to support them to take accountability."

This brings me back to the boundaries work Shawna talks about. How does one reconcile the autonomy, agency, responsibility, and mutuality? What's mine to carry, what's someone else's to carry, and what do we hold collectively? What I'm trying to make room for in my mind and in my heart is that, as organizer and educator Mariame Kaba says, "No one enters violence for the first time by committing it."[9]

8. Mia Mingus, "Pods and Pod Mapping Worksheet," Bay Area Transformative Justice Collective, June 2016, https://batjc.wordpress.com/pods-and-pod-mapping-worksheet.

9. "Thinking about How to Abolish Prisons with Mariame Kaba," April 10, 2019, *Why Is This Happening? with Chris Hayes*, podcast, MP3 audio, https://megaphone.link/NBCN5270192606.

All the hurt and harm we are experiencing *and* causing in the world is from experienced and inherited pain and trauma. I want to heal my own trauma and pain because it brings me closer to being a happy, free person. But it is also the thing that will decrease the harm I do cause, and make it easier for me to hold myself accountable when I mess up. I am committed to doing that work and I can't do it without other people committing to help me.

PEOPLE WERE SAVED BY
THE RELATIONSHIPS THEY BUILT

"We can't build community safety without also building community," Ejeris Dixon told me. The transformative justice approach can be used to intervene once harm has occurred. In her work, Ejeris also creates the networks of people that help keep people safe from harm. When Ejeris began to work on building community safety systems, she started by talking to her mother. Ejeris's mother grew up in New Orleans in the 1940s through '60s in a community that experienced police violence, white nationalist terror, and Jim Crow. They didn't call the police if violence occurred inside their community because the police were often the perpetrators of violence. Instead, an informal network of respected community leaders—teachers, ministers, shop owners, and others—were called upon to address conflict and violence.

Recognizing this history, Ejeris understood that building community safety systems was about reconnecting with an existing cultural practice and shaping it for the present—not inventing something new.

Ejeris helped start the Safe OUTside the System Collective (SOS) at the Audre Lorde Project.[10] SOS was created to organize with queer and trans people of color to create community-based strategies for safety. Part of the work Ejeris did was helping people map out their networks to see where their connections overlapped with others' connections, where there were gaps, and where people lived or worked close to one another. The opportunity to build with potential allies came when one of the people inside the network started getting harassed on their way home from work. Ejeris worked with them to build relationships with the people who were usually present along the route they took home. This work was daunting because it meant coming out to strangers, but ultimately it was effective. "Time and time again, I've known people who were saved by the relationships they built."[11]

Part of why those relationships are important is because, even if you don't object to police or policing, they and other emergency responders are limited in their ability to come to your rescue.

One summer morning I was in my yard watering plants. I heard someone yelling, "Fire, fire!" I ran out to the street to

10. Per their website, "The Audre Lorde Project is a Lesbian, Gay, Bisexual, Two Spirit, Trans and Gender Non Conforming People of Color center for community organizing, focusing on the New York City area. Through mobilization, education and capacity-building, we work for community wellness and progressive social and economic justice. Committed to struggling across differences, we seek to responsibly reflect, represent and serve our various communities." Learn more at https://alp.org/about.

11. Ejeris Dixon, "Building Community Safety: Practical Steps Toward Liberatory Transformation," Truthout, August 25, 2015, https://truthout.org/articles/building-community-safety-practical-steps-toward-liberatory-transformation/.

see my neighbor Tina standing in front of Ms. Z's house as flames shot out of the side window. She wondered aloud if anyone was inside. She'd already called the fire department, but if someone was inside, it was going to be too late for them by the time help arrived. We soon saw the curtain open and a face peek out. It was Ms. Z's adult grandnephew who has mental disabilities. He was clearly making no effort to leave. I ran up the stairs and banged on the door, calling his name. He opened it and retreated back into the house as thick black smoke poured out of the doorway. I went in after him, taking his arm gently and telling him we had to leave. I led him out as things started exploding in the back of the house. I called Ms. Z and broke the news to her that her house was on fire but that her grandnephew was safe. She told me she would be right there. Then, I called Will and Amy, who live next door to her, because it was clear that the fire was going to affect their house too.

Ms. Z and her family lost a lot, and it took more than a year for their house to be rebuilt. But it could have been worse. If her grandnephew didn't know who I was—someone who greets him, someone whose home his little cousins play at, someone his aunt talks to—he wouldn't have opened the door.

Beyond fire, there are any number of other scenarios I can think of where knowing the people around me makes me safer. Maybe it's because I live in California with its unpredictable earthquakes, seasonal fires, and regular droughts. Or maybe it's my consumption of science fiction focused on dystopian futures. Maybe it's climate change, antibiotic-resistant bacteria, wealth inequality, and the rise of fascism and extremism. Whatever it is, I find myself more frequently thinking and talking about the apocalypse. My imagination is not stirred much by surviving the actual precipitating event, but more on how we'd survive afterward. I wonder most about what skills and knowledge we'd need to survive and rebuild society—agricultural, medical, mechanical, artistic, strategic, psychological, spiritual. But the thing I'm most clear on is that no one survives alone. Without the support and company of others, you are doomed. Research on disasters makes this clear.

Daniel Aldrich is a political science professor who studies disasters—Hurricane Katrina, the 2011 Fukushima earthquake, the 2004 Indian Ocean tsunami—and the resilience required to survive them. "Resilience is best understood as a characteristic of communities rather than individuals," Aldrich writes. "Resilience isn't personal grit; it's the capacity of a neighborhood or community to respond, mitigate and adapt to crisis."[12] In his work, he's found that the places that experience the highest survival rates are not the wealthiest or those where individuals have disaster kits, but the places with the strongest social cohesion—where people are most connected to each other. Mimi Kim explained that when violence happens, the people the survivor trusts are the first responders. Aldrich echoes this, explaining that in a disaster, the people around you, such as your neighbors, are the first responders.[13]

12. Daniel Aldrich, "Some Communities Are Destroyed by Tragedy and Disaster. Others Spring Back. Here's What Makes a Difference," *Washington Post*, December 9, 2015, https://www.washingtonpost.com /news/monkey-cage/wp/2015/12/09/some-communities-are-destroyed -by-tragedy-and-disaster-others-spring-back-heres-what-makes-the -difference/?utm_term=.4684bd19829a.

13. Daniel Aldrich, "Recovering from Disasters: Social Networks Matter More Than Bottled Water and Batteries," The Conversation, February 13, 2017, https://theconversation.com/recovering-from-disasters-social-net works-matter-more-than-bottled-water-and-batteries-69611.

If you haven't built trust and connection, you might be on your own.

Capitalism tells us that human beings—our bodies, our homes, our environment—are disposable. It tells us that a bottom line that extracts as much as it can from people while providing them with as little as it can is how you do business.[14] One of the things I appreciate about abolition and transformative justice is that they insist that we value everyone, insist that we are all worthy.

Abolition and transformative justice practices and groups like OCUEJ and Homefullness show us that we can create systems of safety and support that don't reinforce oppression, disconnection, and violence. They tell us how to show up for ourselves, our loved ones, and our neighbors. I think they also speak to how we can show up more broadly for people we don't know.

THE SACRIFICE OF BEES

Bear with me for a minute as I get hella nerdy about honeybees. It's a cliché to talk about bees when talking about community, but I'm going to do it anyway because I'm a bee-keeper and there are some things I've learned firsthand from them about community.

Most bees are solitary, but honeybees are communal. The bees in a honeybee hive are almost entirely female. There's

---

14. It is worth your time to read "In Order to Understand the Brutality of American Capitalism, You Have to Start on the Plantation," a piece Matthew Desmond wrote as part of the *New York Times*'s 1619 project, https://www.nytimes.com/interactive/2019/08/14/magazine/slavery -capitalism.html.

the queen, of course, and then all the worker bees. Drones are the only males. The female bees all have a job to do. The queen lays eggs (sorry, but contrary to popular belief, she's not in charge) and the workers do things like care for larvae, control the temperature of the hive, clean up, guard the hive, collect nectar and pollen, make wax, and feed drones. Drones can't even feed themselves, they just eat and hang out. Initially, I chalked this up to another one of the ways in which nature can be sexist, but then I found out that in the fall, as resources decline, the workers stop feeding drones and kick them out.

There's plenty that's not worth imitating about honeybee society. The queen is basically a kept breeder who lives or dies depending on how good a job she's doing—the workers will just make a new queen if they aren't pleased with her. And while I love that they are matriarchal, kicking out the males to starve when resources get low is not something I'm ready to get behind. What is worth contemplating is the ways in which honeybees are deeply interdependent with the bees in their hives, and each hive with the hives around them.

Since beekeeping is not your typical hobby, my friends often take a little pride in including it in their introductions of me. They'll say, "Mia makes honey." I am quick to clarify that I actually steal honey. Bees make honey for themselves because it's what they eat. When I harvest it, I'm stealing some of their food. As you might imagine, they do not fucking like this at all. When I harvest honey, despite my efforts to be gentle and work carefully, I usually get attacked by guard bees. The tone of their buzz says, "You're going to catch these hands" and then they fly repeatedly and directly at my face.

I've also been chased out of my yard by guard bees during

robbing season. In the Bay Area there's not a lot blooming in the late summer, and strong hives will rob weaker ones for honey. Just as the bees do not like it when I take their honey, they do not like being robbed by other bees. It makes them generally agitated and less tolerant of potential threats. If I wander into my yard when they've been fending off attack, they chase me away (especially if I'm wearing black, which is almost always, because they think I might be a bear—this is why beekeepers wear white!).

These tiny insects are fierce as hell. Imagine being that small and chasing something as large as a human to defend your people. As you may know, worker bees' stingers are barbed, so if they sting you, the stinger and venom sac stay in your flesh, their innards get pulled out, and they die. They give their lives to protect their hive.

Then there's the whole drone situation. When a queen is born, she flies off to a place called a drone congregation area (seriously). Dudes are hanging out, sometimes in the thousands, to get laid. (I imagine a combination of a middle school dance, a hipster bar, and a cruisey park.) Queens hook up with ten to twenty drones, who die after mating. The queen flies back to her hive with her pockets full of sperm so she can fulfill her job—laying eggs. She won't mate with the bees from her own hive because, ew, those are her brothers. All hives raise drones, but they do it to ensure the biodiversity of hundreds of other hives around them. And they benefit from other hives raising the drones that their queen will mate with.

These two aspects of honeybee life—the risking of self to protect one's home community and expending resources for the benefit of the broader community—I find instructional.

For humans, the idea that we would do labor or give up resources without direct benefit requires having faith that the universe will attend to our generosity. Our culture of winning, getting ahead, and zero-sum gains does not support this kind of mind-set. It's more than the idea of self-sacrifice as a practice you benefit from because it makes you feel righteous or earns you points with your god. It's also about recognizing that our collective survival depends on understanding that there is enough for all of us and we don't need to hoard resources at the expense of others (hello, billionaires). We don't have the benefit of the clearly drawn lines from action to impact that bees have. But I've experienced something like this.

A couple of years ago, I decided to be more intentional about spending my money, social capital, access, and time on Black womxn.[15] I did this for several reasons, the first and most important being that I am unapologetically about Black womxn being centered in so much of the social justice work I do, it only made sense that I extend this to other parts of my life. Black womxn are systematically under-resourced, under-credited, exploited, and underestimated. It benefits us and everyone else, if we are able to live to our full potential. If I learn of an opportunity, I forward it to Black womxn. If I need a service or particular product, I look for a Black womxn to give my money to. I reserve my (limited) philanthropic giving to causes that directly benefit Black womxn. I reserve unpaid opportunities to "pick my brain" for Black womxn.

---

15. In an effort to have a word that stands in a longer list of gender identities—gender queer, gender nonbinary, gender nonconforming, along with cis and transgender women, some folks replace the *e* in *women* with an *x* to expand its meaning.

Since I started doing it, I've noticed it coming back to me in the form of things like new work, bouquets of flowers, love notes, encouragement and appreciation, free stuff, introductions to funders, and speaking gigs. What's so powerful about this is that all these benefits and resources are often not from the womxn whom I've supported.

As for giving up my life, there are only two people I would knowingly sacrifice my life for—my kids—but I would *risk* my safety and resources for a lot of people, strangers in some cases.

OTHER PEOPLE ARE OURS TO CARE FOR

The summer between my sophomore and junior year of college, I lived in my friend Whitney's mom's apartment in Brooklyn Heights. I had a temporary job doing in-person interviews as part of a massive health research project that Harlem Hospital was conducting. After work, I'd take the train from Harlem to Brooklyn. Sometimes, I'd go out after work and come home late. One night I noticed a man on the platform as I waited for the train home. He was wearing a bulky coat and a hat, way too much clothing for the humid, hot weather. He walked up to a woman who was sitting on a bench. He was standing too close to her and muttering. She was doing her best to ignore him. Then the train came and she got up and he moved away. I got on the train. Very few people got off the train with me in Brooklyn Heights. As I walked down the platform toward the stairs I saw the man I'd seen before approaching a man in a suit. He was, again, muttering and standing too close. The suit man was gently responding and kept backing up to create space, but the muttering man got more agitated and kept moving closer until eventually the suit man was cornered. I was the only other person around. I started to walk up the stairs just a few feet away from them, listening to their interaction. I stopped at the top and turned around. Without much thought, I sighed with as much loud exasperation as I could, and hollered down the stairs, "Alex, let's go. We're already late." Both men looked up at me. I looked at "Alex"/suit man, and said, "We're late. C'mon." He, not quite following my storyline, walked quickly around the muttering man and said, "Hey! How's it going? It's good to see you." We exited the station together and he thanked me. We went our separate ways.

At the time, I didn't wonder why I did that, but now I think it was part of my deep desire to practice an ethic that says if I want to live in a world where we show up for others when they need it, I have to do my part. Now that I'm older and my politics are sharper, I imagine that my approach would be focused on helping the muttering man as well as the man in the suit.

There's that famous poem by Martin Niemöller, a German pastor: "First they came for the communists, and I did not speak out because I was not a communist." He goes on to include trade unionists and Jews before he is left alone with no one to speak for him because they are all disappeared or dead. As a younger person, I appreciated this slightly admonishing poem because I knew that as a Black woman I was more likely to be in the place of the communist than the person at the end who is left with no one to defend them. It seemed like Niemöller was putting forward a practical calculation as much as a moral urgency. Now, I feel more accord with James Baldwin's "An Open Letter to My Sister, Miss Angela Davis."[16]

In November 1970, Davis was standing trial for murder and kidnapping (for which she was acquitted). Baldwin wrote the letter while he was in Istanbul directing a play. In it he articulates the separation white Americans create from their own humanity. "They will never, so long as their whiteness puts so sinister a distance between themselves and their own experience and the experience of others, feel themselves sufficiently human, sufficiently worthwhile, to become responsible for themselves, their leaders, their country, their children, or their fate." He also voices a sibling sentiment to Niemöller's writing:

"Some of us, white and black, know how great a price has already been paid to bring into existence a new consciousness, a new people, an unprecedented nation. If we know, and do nothing, we are worse than the murderers hired in our name.

"If we know, then we must fight for your life as though it were our own—which it is—and render impassable with our bodies the corridor to the gas chamber. For, if they take you in the morning, they will be coming for us that night."

Niemöller, a Lutheran pastor, was not a communist or trade unionist or Jew and his point was about the responsibility we have to show up for people who are not us. And Baldwin was recognizing that those who risk themselves on the front lines are actively protecting us. Niemöller says, in

---

16. James Baldwin, "An Open Letter to My Sister, Miss Angela Davis," *New York Review of Books*, January 7, 1971, https://www.nybooks.com /articles/1971/01/07/an-open-letter-to-my-sister-miss-angela-davis/.

standing up for others, we ensure that others will be around
to stand up for us. And Baldwin says others are already standing up for us, so it's our duty to stand up for them.

All the horrors we face today will only be solved if we understand that we are all in this together. We are most moved
toward action by our relationships with others. But we aren't
all going to have relationships with people who are, today,
to paraphrase Baldwin, paying a great price to raise our consciousness, forge a better America, and save us all. Yet we
need to show up anyway. We need to develop a sense of belonging in and to the world that tells us other people are ours
to care for.

Safety is each of us having the things we need to live a
life of well-being—food, shelter, education, health care, love,
and connection. These are human rights that should be accessible to all of us. Walls, weapons, and prisons fundamentally work against our ability to have those things. Our social
contracts need to be strengthened and infused with Harriet
Tubman/Audre Lorde/Toni Cade Bambara–type love if we
have any hope of saving ourselves. The love of those heroes,
as Savannah Shange, assistant professor of anthropology and
critical race studies, explained to me, is deep and fierce, but
not unconditional or without discernment. They "love powerfully *while demanding* accountability and respect."

HOW WE SHOW UP

WHITNEY KIMBALL COE lives in Athens, Tennessee, with her husband and kids, where she works at the Center for Rural Strategies. Athens is a very small town of under fourteen thousand people. "I was at church and my friend Becky came up to me and she said, 'Nelson is reading a book that he got from the library this week and he found a bookmark in it and he thinks it's yours.' And I was like, 'What book's he reading?' She told me what it was and I said, 'Oh yeah. I just turned that one back in.' And she brought it back to me. It was this really special bookmark somebody had made for me and in the corner of it, it had my initials, WKC. Nelson, her husband, knows that I read. We have one public library and he made all those connections when he saw that bookmark."

Whitney has lived in, and travels to, cities, but she has, I think, a calling to work in rural America, both to help it thrive but also to protect what is unique about it, things she thinks those of us who live in cities and suburbs could learn from. In Athens, where her parents met and she grew up, there is a kind of familiarity everyone has with one another. There's one gym, one post office, one coffee shop, one grocery store, one library, and one community theater, so people of different political parties, races, classes, and ages are regularly interacting with one another.

"Even though we haven't necessarily had conversations about reconciliation, we have to be integrated because we're all using these spaces. Our proximity to one another helps us untangle some of those disagreements and some of the partisanship." Whitney, who is white, is quick to point out that this "integration" doesn't mean people have figured out how to reconcile power dynamics and political tensions.

The fact that there's only one of everything means you can't be one person at your kid's school and another person at work, because your coworkers' kids all go to school with your kids. "That is so freeing in some ways because you kind of just have to go for it. You can only constrain yourself to a point without going nuts." Being relentlessly known terrifies us, but I think we also crave the freedom of it. If you can't hide yourself, at some point you just have to be, like, "Fuck it." Whitney says, "It's treatment for the existential loneliness we all experience no matter where we live."

She also admits that it can be smothering, like when people go through a personal transformation and those they've known all their life still see them as they were before. "But I do think that there are many examples of people who have grown up in a community and hardships have happened to them, terrible things have happened to them, or they've done terrible things and yet they continue to live there. Over time that becomes part of the fabric of the story of that place. And they continue to make it be meaningful."

I think about the relationships I've outgrown—because of my personal or political evolution—and how living in cities has meant I could let go of those relationships and form new ones. Whitney makes me wonder if that was the easy way out. I don't think relationships need to be held on to forever just because they exist. Plenty of us have rightly freed ourselves from old relationships because people just couldn't accept who we are. But maybe I've been too impatient and unforgiving when people who love and care about me are moving at a different pace or in a different direction. I wonder who I've left behind that I could have brought along. I also wonder who has let *me* go because I couldn't see their growth or was lagging behind. I hope I can get better at offering more patience and grace to my loved ones, as I no doubt need that myself.

FULL AND FED

The Reverend Jennifer Bailey is the epitome of grace. She grew up in Quincy, Illinois, a town of forty thousand that is about 90 percent white and 10 percent people of color. Quincy's Bethel African Methodist Episcopal (AME) Church was instrumental in Jennifer's formation.

"It was the one place in my life where I was taught that being Black was good. It was the one place where I was affirmed as being beautiful and beloved in the eyesight of this thing we call God. It was in Reverend Pendleton's pulpit that I heard a narrative about Black folks and Black history that I wasn't learning in my classroom in that predominantly white context. So my teachers were people like Reverend Pendleton, or Mrs. Pendleton, his wife, who was this lady in my church who was just an incredible educator by training, and people like Ms. Jackie Watson, who was our church secretary, who made the bulletins and the dinner rolls for our spaghetti dinner. Or Ms. Green, who was nosy but always had people in order, and my mom, who was president of the Missionary Society. I learned about not just the politics of the church, but the politics of gender and the politics of race."

In church, Jennifer learned the power in Black women claiming autonomy and authority. She also learned about community. And these two things—the power of Black women and the holding and care of community—were inextricably linked because it was Black women who she saw nurturing, feeding, and taking little while making much. "I learned about the importance of lineage in those spaces. Cooking in those spaces, or bearing witness to the cooking that was happening, became a way to pass down our history through the little food that we were making. What I learned about community was the importance of lineage in a world that would seek to erase your history. There are subversive ways that, through recipes, we can tell stories that the history books I had in my classroom were not necessarily telling me."

In her church, as she grew, she went from being fed to delivering meals to Black elders in the town. That led her to the food justice movement, and eventually to becoming ordained and building the Faith Matters Network.

"My day job focuses on three things: healing, spiritual growth, and connection for faith leaders, organizers, and activists who often find themselves on the front lines of struggle, and who, by the very nature of their positions, are often not poured into. They're the ones pouring out to others and sacrificing themselves for community. We're figuring out how we can create those conditions through which folks feel fully full and fully fed, knowing that there's going to be something that depletes you."

This is a question I want to ask myself and my own community more—what conditions make us feel full and fed? Creating community is creating culture—practice, ritual, social norms. What does that creation need to look like so we are not just filled up when we are depleted but live a life that is less depleting?

I spent much of my childhood and twenties working, learning, and sometimes socializing in environments where I felt like I had to wear armor all the time to protect myself from sometimes hostile and sometimes well-meaning racism, sexism, and classism. That armor is heavy and I spent enough time wearing it that it was preventing me from being my full self and growing in all the ways I could have. So, in my thirties, I stopped spending as much time in those spaces. I created a bubble for myself of relationships where the humanity and value and dignity of people who are Black and female and queer and any other host of marginalized identities was not a question. We still disagree plenty and have different perspectives on a host of things. But these are the people with whom I can be my whole self. These are the people who push me to heal and grow, and with whom I feel safe enough to do so.

Living in my bubble is important for my well-being and it's the place we practice world making—creating some version of the future world we want to live in now, in the present. Living into the future, creating the culture we want with the people closest to us, is a declaration of love and commitment.

I still spend time working with people who are less like me in identity or ideology or understanding. But my armor is lighter because I'm stronger. It's like my people helped me discover my superpowers. It makes it possible for me to do the work I'm called to do with people outside my bubble—revealing our often hidden connections.

We are living in a contradiction—we are made for inter-dependence, connection, and love, but part of a culture that espouses the opposite. Creating and keeping what is counter-culture requires vigilance. We stumble, backslide, and forget. There is a tension between existing in one world while trying to live into another one. That place in between them is full of friction. But like so many change processes, the thing we are trying to get to holds the key to getting there. Reclaiming and reinventing family, friendship, and community is a pro-cess we do *with our family, friends, and community.*

As the stories in this book show us, there's no singular way to do this, but it requires thought, deliberation, and cour-age. In my work life, I've learned to create strategic plans and steps, and benchmarks. That sounds counterintuitive to how we build connection, but maybe that's part of what we need now—Saqib and Aisha's spreadsheets, my sticky notes, Lawrence's friendship zones, Homefulness's manifesto. Cal-endars, reminders, and video messaging apps.

There has to be something organic and serendipitous about it too. When Akaya created a container for our New Universal gathering, we followed our hearts, spirits, and in-tuition inside it to discover one another and create song, joy, laughter, and healing. When Nwamaka and I started Black Women's Freedom Circle, we had agendas, but eventually we let that fall away to the collective wisdom of the group's leadership. We can attune ourselves to opportunities to come closer instead of stay isolated, to reach out instead of do nothing, to say, "I'm here! Come play with me, come know me, come let me see you."

Finding and strengthening connection is a craft, not a science, but there are common denominators, patterns, and guideposts. And I think that if we look inside ourselves and those closest to us, we will find that we have most of the tools and materials, and can figure out how we might put them together.

Maybe it is not even something we need to construct. To paraphrase an idea from john a. powell, who leads the UC Berkeley Othering & Belonging Institute, we don't build connection because we are fundamentally connected. I find that perspective reassuring. The American Dream makes us complicit in building barriers to our fundamental connection. It tries to keep us apart by telling us that we are out here on our own. That means our work is to become more aware of what's already there and peel back the delusion of separateness to reveal our interdependence.

It has weighed heavily on me since I started writing this book that we are living through a time of great polarization in the United States and in other parts of the world, and the very present impact of climate change and fascism. When I hear about the number of species going extinct, the melting of the polar ice caps, the victory of yet another fascist leader, attacks on democracy, brazen displays of racism, or the passage of a discriminatory law, I sometimes think, *Well, humans, we had a good run, but I think we're just about done. And clearly the earth will be better off without us.* It's hard to keep the fear, anger, and frustration from making a home in me, leaving me despondent, bitter, and mean-spirited.

And yet I ultimately always circle back to hope, because shit, what else is there? If we give up, we *definitely* lose. Trying is the only option.

My conversation with the Reverend Jennifer Bailey circled around to redemption and what that means in the context of being part of a broader community. She said, "Although I come from a particular space of faith commitment, and have a particular belief of the divine, what we're talking about is the bigger question of how we're human together in these times. Part of the call of this age is to learn how to accompany one another and answer the bigger question—particularly in the American context of how we want to do this life thing together, because we're at a critical crossroads."

Our job is not to force people toward redemption. We can't make them atone. But can we hold on to the idea that everyone is redeemable? "There's the concept within Christianity of the Imago Dei," Jen explained to me, "that we are all created in this divine image of God. I've found that to be a real challenge to my faith on a regular basis. And I actually believe that all people are created in God's image. I actually believe that, as that is a core tenet of my theological grounding and understanding in this worldview. That means that I need to find the divine spark in Donald Trump, right? And when I need a good test in my faith, I ask myself that question, do I see Donald Trump as someone who is redeemable? If my answer is no, then, and I use this language quite literally in terms of the actual practical definition of it, I am a heretic."

How do I recognize the divine spark in everyone? It's easy for me to hold the divinity of my children and husband, of my dearest people. It is much harder for me to see divinity in people who behave with cruelty or stinginess, people who are being rude or dishonest. But I easily slip into a good people–bad people binary when I ask myself this question. That binary is one of the things that obscures our connection. What

Jen is really asking doesn't stop with the challenge of believing in the humanity of people who say and do evil things. I think it asks us to see our own divinity and to believe in the possibility of our own redemption. Because we have to believe we can redeem ourselves if we are to keep ourselves alive on this planet.

NEW UNIVERSAL

The New Universal met a second time in September 2019. On our first day, Akaya told us that in addition to standing on the shoulders of our ancestors whose strength and conviction was supporting and propelling us forward, we are also being led by our descendants.

On the third day, I led us in an exercise that put us in touch with a descendant.[1] We sat in a circle in a round cabin with vaulted ceilings and windows all around us. I had us imagine a child descendant of ours (biological or chosen) five generations in the future who was living in the world of our most positive, joyful, whole imagination. I love how this process frees my mind to dream with courage, boldness, hope, and joy. This process allows you to envision what you want and hold it up in contrast to what you have. Then you can identify the places in your life that you can shift to align with the future you want.

---

1. The exercise I developed was inspired by one I participated in during Transitions Lab, which you read about in Chapter 2. Julie Quiroz, who facilitated it, adapted it from a story by Alexis Pauline Gumbs in *Octavia's Brood: Science Fiction Stories from Social Justice Movements* (Edinburgh: AK Press, 2015).

We don't get to the future we want by following a linear path plotted out from point A to B to C. The future we want is a spark inside us that says yes to joy and laughter and pleasure. It says yes to creativity and art and music. It says yes to transformative healing and care, and I am because we are. It says yes to vulnerability and our collective well-being and love. The more we fan and feed it, the more it sustains and grows. It lives in us and then we live in it and—✳—the future is here. We get to the future we want by practicing it now.

During this second New Universal gathering, our baseline was joy. During waking hours, from almost anywhere at the retreat center, you could hear our unrestrainable laughter. Our collective energy was like a river running through everything. We were not the only group at the retreat center where we gathered. I was struck by the response to our undeniable presence. Some people chose to allow the waters of our warmth, care, and kindness wash over them. Some did not. The latter seemed to recede, while the former seemed to grow brighter—fully full and fully fed. The first time we gathered, I went home understanding that we could conjure the future, just by being in each other's presence for a few days. This time, I went home realizing what now seems obvious. A culture where liberatory joy, love, and belonging is foundational is powerfully attractive to those who want it. And it's threatening to those who don't. Those who hold tightly to the last gasps of the old American Dream will fade into the past.

I know that the way to create the world we want, and the one we owe those who come after us, is only something that can be achieved in community. I am excited by a future in which all of us is cared for and loved so deeply that we give freely of ourselves to others because we are fully full and fully fed, and we know that our well-being is dependent on the well-being of those around us. I also know that while I keep circling back to hope and doing my part to build that world, I also fear what's coming. Massive change is happening and it will be inevitably increasingly hard and painful, and many of us will get lost along the way. The only protection against the worst-case scenario is also in community.

We need each other. Either way and always.

GRATITUDE

I AM GRATEFUL TO everyone who participated in making this book. Thank you for sharing your personal stories, giving me suggestions and edits, providing me with places to write, sending me supportive texts, mailing me chocolate, listening to me talk endlessly about connection and friendship, sitting quietly next to me while I worked, and celebrating every milestone. I've thanked you all personally. I'm not naming any of you all here, to protect identities. If you helped me out and don't feel properly thanked, please hit me up and I will send you a personal note of appreciation.

Public gratitude goes to my editors Renée Sedliar, who cheerleaded, reassured, pushed, wrangled, prompted, and shepherded this book's entire process, and Cynthia Greenlee who provided critical, loving deep edits and reflections.

Public gratitude also goes to my husband, Nino, and our kids, who supported me in making this book with their endless encouragement, hugs, food, and so much love, but also sacrificed a lot of time and care so I could have the solitude I needed to write. You all are the best.

In those moments of solitude I was never alone. Thank you to my ancestors, gods, orisha, and plant and nonhuman animal relations for your powerful presence.

Thank you, prosecco, apples, and chocolate.

Thank you to my parents, Georgia Whitney and Maurice Hope Thompson, and my grandmother, Florence Icilda Thompson, for my inheritance of words.

RESOURCES

No list of resources could capture the work of everyone who informed my thinking for this book. This is a sample of the books and articles I found valuable, even if I didn't agree with them.

Books

Bergman, Carla, and Nick Montgomery. *Joyful Militancy: Building Thriving Resistance in Toxic Times*. Baltimore: AK Press, 2017.

brown, adrienne maree. *Pleasure Activism: The Politics of Feeling Good*. Edinburgh: AK Press, 2019.

DePaulo, Bella. *How We Live Now: Redefining Home and Family in the 21st Century*. New York: Atria Books/Beyond Words, 2015.

DiAngelo, Robin. *White Fragility: Why It's So Hard for White People to Talk About Racism*. Boston: Beacon Press, 2018.

Dixon, Ejeris, and Leah Lakshmi Piepzna-Samarasinha, eds. *Beyond Survival: Strategies and Stories from the Transformative Justice Movement*. Baltimore: AK Press, 2020.

Gilmore, Ruth Wilson. *Golden Gulag: Prisons, Surplus, Crisis, and Opposition in Globalizing California*. Oakland: University of California Press, 2007.

Hunter, Tera W. *To 'Joy My Freedom: Southern Black Women's Lives and Labors After the Civil War*. Cambridge, MA: Harvard University Press, 1997.

Kendi, Ibram X. *Stamped from the Beginning: The Definitive History of Racist Ideas in America*. New York: Nation Books, 2016.

Lieberman, Matthew D. *Social: Why Our Brains Are Wired to Connect*. New York: Broadway Books, 2013.

Martin, Courtney E. *The New Better Off: Reinventing the American Dream*. Berkeley, CA: Seal Press, 2016.

McClain, Dani. *We Live for the We: The Political Power of Black Motherhood*. New York: Bold Type Books, 2019.

Oluo, Ijeoma. *So You Want to Talk About Race*. New York: Seal Press, 2018.

Samaran, Nora. *Turn This World Inside Out: The Emergence of Nurturance Culture*. Baltimore: AK Press, 2019.

Schulman, Sarah. *Conflict Is Not Abuse: Overstating Harm, Community Responsibility, and the Duty of Repair*. Vancouver, BC: Arsenal Pulp Press, 2016.

Williams, Rev. Angel Kyodo, and Lama Rod Owens, with Jasmine Syedullah. *Radical Dharma: Talking Race, Love, and Liberation*. Berkeley, CA: North Atlantic Books, 2016.

Articles

Amezcua, Tasha, Ejeris Dixon, and Che J. Rene Long. "Ten Lessons for Creating Safety Without Police." Truthout. https://truthout.org/articles/10-lessons-for-creating-safety-without-the-police-a-reflection-on-the-10-year-anniversary-of-the-sos-collective.

Barriner, Lawrence II. "Why I'm Putting EVERYONE in the Friend Zone." https://medium.com/@lqb2/planning-out-my-friend-ecosystem-95175246458d.

Brown, Sherronda J. "Romance Is Not the Only Type of Black Love That Matters." Black Youth Project. http://blackyouthproject.com/romance-not-black-love-matters.

Brown, Stacia L. "Toni Morrison Taught Me That I Owe Myself My Whole Self." *Washington Post*. https://www.washingtonpost.com/opinions/2019/08/07/toni-morrison-taught-me-that-i-didnt-have-choose-between-art-motherhood.

Crosslin, Siobhan. "On Queerplatonic Relationships, from Someone Who's Actually in One." https://siobhancrosslin.wordpress.com/2017/08/05/on-queerplatonic-relationships-from-someone-whos-actually-in-one.

Crosswell, Marie S. "'Life Partner' Is Not Synonymous with 'Romantic Partner.'" The Good Men Project. https://goodmenproject

.com/gender-sexuality/life-partner-is-not-synonymous-with
-romantic-partner-jvinc.

Dixon, Ejeiris. "Building Community Safety: Practical Steps Toward
Liberatory Transformation." Truthout. https://truthout.org
/articles/building-community-safety-practical-steps-toward
-liberatory-transformation/.

Franklin, Ruth. "John Wray's Clubhouse." Vulture. https://www
.vulture.com/2018/10/john-wray-godsend-camp-cedar-pines.html.

Greene, Mark. "Why Men Need Platonic Touch." Uplift. https://
upliftconnect.com/why-men-need-platonic-touch.

Jeppesen, Sandra. "Queering Heterosexuality." The Anarchist Library.
https://theanarchistlibrary.org/library/sandra-jeppesen-queering
-heterosexuality.

Lakshmin, Pooja, MD. "We Don't Need Self-Care; We Need Boundaries." OpMed. https://opmed.doximity.com/articles/we-don-t
-need-self-care-we-need-boundaries.

"Lost Friends." Advertisements from the *Southwestern Christian Advocate.* https://www.hnoc.org/database/lost-friends/index.html.

Luna, Caleb. "Romantic Love Is Killing Us: Who Takes Care of Us
When We Are Single?" The Body Is Not an Apology. https://the
bodyisnotanapology.com/magazine/romantic-love-is-killing-us.

McCrea, Aisling. "Self-Care Won't Save Us." Current Affairs. https://
www.currentaffairs.org/2018/11/self-care-wont-save-us.

Metzl, Jonathan M. "Dying of Whiteness." *Boston Review.* http://
bostonreview.net/race/jonathan-m-metzl-dying-whiteness.

Mingus, Mia. "How to Give a Good Apology." Leaving Evidence.
https://leavingevidence.wordpress.com/2019/12/18/how-to
-give-a-good-apology-part-1-the-four-parts-of-accountability.

Perry, David M. "How Disabled People Care for Each Other When
Doctors Can't." *Pacific Standard.* https://psmag.com/social-justice
/how-disabled-people-care-for-each-other-when-doctors-cant.

Prevost, Shelley. "Build a 'Moai' for Better Relationships, Longer Life."
NoogaToday. https://noogatoday.6amcity.com/build-a-moai-for
-better-relationships-longer-life/.

Saint Louis, Catherine. "Debunking Myths About Estrangement."
New York Times. https://www.nytimes.com/2017/12/20/well
/family/debunking-myths-about-estrangement.html.

Schwartz, Alexandra. "Love Is Not a Permanent State of Enthusi-
     asm: An Interview with Esther Perel." *New Yorker.* https://www
     .newyorker.com/culture/the-new-yorker-interview/love-is-not
     -a-permanent-state-of-enthusiasm-an-interview-with-esther
     -perel.
Shulevitz, Judith. "Why You Never See Your Friends Anymore." *At-
     lantic.* https://www.theatlantic.com/magazine/archive/2019/11
     /why-dont-i-see-you-anymore/598336.
Tannen, Deborah. "Women's Friendships, in Sickness and in Health."
     New York Times. https://www.nytimes.com/2017/04/25/well
     /family/womens-friendships-in-sickness-and-in-health.html.
Thompson, Derek. "Workism Is Making Americans Miserable."
     Atlantic. https://www.theatlantic.com/ideas/archive/2019/02
     /religion-workism-making-americans-miserable/583441.
Trimble, Megan. "'Traditional Masculinity' Is Harmful to Boys,
     Men." *US News and World Report.* https://www.usnews.com
     /news/national-news/articles/2019-01-09/traditional-masculinity
     -is-harmful-to-boys-men-american-psychological-association
     -says.

INDEX

ABOUT THE AUTHOR

M IA IS A pathfinder, community curator, and storyteller who steadily engages the leadership and wisdom of people experiencing injustice to chart new visions of American life. She has a gift for making visible and leveraging the brilliance of everyday people so that our collective gifts reach larger spheres of influence, effect cultural and political change, and create well-being for everyone.

In *More Than Enough*, her podcast miniseries from The Nation, she expands the current guaranteed income movement by tapping into the voices and visions of low-income people. Previously, as founding codirector of Family Story, Mia lifted up a new national story about what makes a good family. As vice president of the Family Independence Initiative, she leveraged the power of data and stories to illuminate and accelerate the initiative low-income families take to improve their lives.

Her public conversations, from the New America series centering Black women as agents of change to her 2015 TED talk "The Story We Tell About Poverty Isn't True," draw targeted attention to the stories of people who are finding their way into leadership roles despite myriad barriers, while also highlighting the vibrant terrain of all marginalized people who are leading on the ground and solving for tomorrow.

Mia is a senior fellow of the Economic Security Project. She was an inaugural Ascend Fellow and faculty member with the Aspen Institute, a New American California Fellow, and advocate-in-residence with University of Pennsylvania's School of Social Policy and Practice. Mia lives and dreams big on the occupied land of the Chochenyo Ohlone people (a.k.a. Oakland, California).